# Conjunctions and Disjunctions

# OCTAVIO PAZ

# Conjunctions and Disjunctions

ARCADE PUBLISHING • NEW YORK

First Skyhorse Publishing Edition 2015

Originally published in Mexico by Joaquín Mortiz, S.A., under the title *Conjunciones y Disyunciones*.

First published in the United States as a Richard Seaver Book / The Viking Press in 1974 by The Viking Press, Inc.

First Seaver Books paperback edition 1982

First Arcade Edition 1990

Acknowledgment is made to The Macmillian Company, M.B. Yeats, Macmillan of Bassingstoke & London, Macmillan Co. of Canada for material from Collected Poems of William Butler Years, © Macmillian Company 1956.

Arcade Publishing books may be purchased in bulk at special discounts for sales promotion, corporate gifts, fund-raising, or educational purposes. Special editions can also be created to specifications. For details, contact the Special Sales Department, Arcade Publishing, 307 West 36th Street, 11th Floor, New York, NY 10018 or arcade@skyhorsepublishing.com.

Arcade Publishing® is a registered trademark of Skyhorse Publishing, Inc.®, a Delaware corporation.

Visit our website at www.arcadepub.com.

10 9 8 7 6 5 4 3 2 1

Library of Congress Cataloging-in-Publication Data is available on file.

Cover design by Owen Corrigan

Print ISBN: 978-1-62872-532-2
Ebook ISBN: 978-1-62872-171-3

Printed in the United States of America

*The Phenomenon,*
engraving by José Guadalupe Posada
(Mexico, Instituto Nacional de Bellas Artes)

*The Toilet of Venus,* Velázquez (London, National Gallery). *Photo: National Gallery*

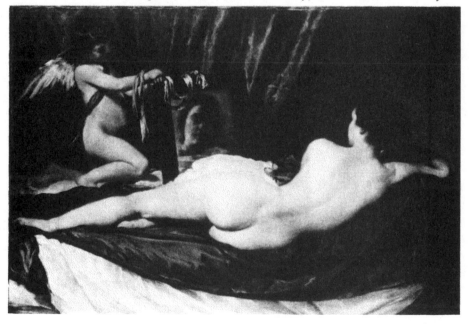

# Contents

# 1 | The Metaphor

There is a woodcut by Posada that shows a figure in a circus: a dwarf seen from the back, but with his face turned toward the spectator, and shown with another face down by his buttocks. Quevedo is no less explicit, and one of his juvenile works bears the title *Gracias y Desgracias del Ojo del Culo* [*Graces and Disgraces of the Eye of the Ass*]. It is a long comparison between an ass and a face. The superiority of the former lies in its having only one eye, as did the Cyclopes that "descended from the gods of sight."

Posada's woodcut and Quevedo's metaphor seem to say the same thing: that asses and faces are identical. There is a difference nonetheless: the woodcut shows that the ass is a face, whereas Quevedo affirms that the ass is like the face of the Cyclopes. We pass from the human world to the mythological world: if the face is bestial, as is the ass, the bestiality of both is divine or demoniacal. If we want to know what the face of the Cyclopes is like, the best thing is to ask Góngora. Let us listen to Polyphemus as he looks in the water and discovers his face:

miréme y lucir vi un sol en mi frente
cuando en el cielo un ojo se veía
neutra el agua dudaba a cual fe preste:
o al cielo humano o al cíclope celeste.

[I looked at myself and saw a sun shining in my forehead
while an eye was visible in the sky
the neutral water doubted which was real:
the human sky or the celestial Cyclops.]

Polyphemus sees his deformed face as *another* firmament. Transformations: the "eye" of the ass—that of the Cyclops—that of the sky. The sun dissolves the face-ass, soul-body dualism in a single dazzling, total image. We regain our former unity, but this unity is neither animal nor human; it is Cyclopean, mythical.

There is not much purpose in repeating here everything that psychoanalysis has taught us about the conflict between the face and the ass, the (repressive) reality principle and the (explosive) pleasure principle. I will merely note here that the metaphor that I mentioned, both as it works upward and as it works downward—the ass as a face and the face as an ass—serves each of these principles alternately. At first, the metaphor uncovers a similarity; then, immediately afterward, it covers it up again, either because the first term absorbs the second, or vice versa. In any case, the similarity disappears and the opposition between ass and face reappears, in a form that is now even stronger than before. Here, too, the similarity at first seems unbearable to us—

and therefore we either laugh or cry; in the second step, the opposition also becomes unbearable—and therefore we either laugh or cry. When we say that the ass is like another face, we deny the soul-body dualism; we laugh because we have resolved the discord that we are. But the victory of the pleasure principle does not last long; at the same time that our laughter celebrates the reconciliation of the soul and the body, it dissolves it and makes it laughable once again. As a matter of fact, the ass is sober-sided; the organs of laughter are the same as those of language: the tongue and the lips. When we laugh at our ass—that caricature of our face—we affirm our separation and bring about the total defeat of the pleasure principle. Our face laughs at our ass and thus retraces the dividing line between the body and the spirit.

Neither the phallus nor the ass has a sense of humor. Being sullen, they are aggressive. Their aggressiveness is the result of the smiling repression of the face. As Baudelaire discovered, long before Freud: smiles, and the comic in general, are the stigmata of original sin, or, to put the matter another way, they are the attributes of our humanity, the result of and the witness to our violent separation from the natural world. The smile is the sign of our duality; if at times we make fun of our own selves with the same acrimony with which we laugh at others every day, it is because we are in fact always two: the I and the other. But the violent emissions of the phallus, the convulsions of the vulva, and the explosions of the ass wipe the smile off our face. Our principles totter, shaken by a psychic earthquake no less powerful than earthquakes in the ground beneath our feet. Deeply disturbed by the violence of our sensations and mental images, we pass from seriousness to hearty laughter. The I and the other become one, and what is more, the I is possessed by the other. Hearty laughter is similar to the physical and psychological spasm: we burst out laughing. This explosion is the contrary of the smile, and I am not certain that it can be called comic. The comic spirit implies two persons: the one who is watching and the one who is being watched, whereas when we laugh heartily the distinction is erased or at least diminished. A burst of laughter not only suppresses the duality, it also obliges us to become one with laughter in general, with the great physiological and cosmic turmoil of the ass and the phallus—the volcano and the monsoon.

A burst of laughter is also a metaphor: the face becomes a phallus, a vulva, or an ass. On the psychological level a burst of laughter is the equivalent of what the expressions of poets and satirists are on the verbal level. Its explosion is an exaggeration that is no less extreme than Góngora's poetic image and Quevedo's wit. Both are the doubles of physiological and cosmic violence. The result is a transmutation: we leap from the world of duality, ruled by the reality principle, into that of the myth of original unity. A fit of laughter is not merely a response to the pleasure principle, nor its copy or reproduction (even though it is both these things): it is the metaphor of pleasure. Hearty laughter is a (provisional) synthesis between the soul and body, the I and the other. This synthesis is a transformation or symbolic translation: we are like the Cyclopes once again. Once again: hearty laughter is a regression to a former state; we return to the world of our own childhood, either individual or collective, to myth and play. We return to the primordial unity —before there was a *you* and an *I*—in the form of a *we* that embraces every living being and every element.

The other response to carnal violence is seriousness, impassivity. This is the philosophical response, as the burst of laughter is the mythical response. Seriousness is an attribute of ascetics and libertines. Hearty laughter is a relaxation, asceticism a rigidity: it hardens the body so as to preserve the soul. I couple the libertine with the ascetic because libertinage is also a hardening, of the spirit first of all, and then of the senses. An asceticism in reverse. With his usual acuity, Sade states that the libertine philosopher must be imperturbable and aspire to the insensibility of the ancient Stoics, to ataraxia. His erotic archetypes are stones, metals, cooled lava. Equivalences, equations: the phallus and the volcano, the vulva and the crater. Resembling an earthquake in his emotional ardor and fury, the libertine must be hard, as stony as the rocks and crags that cover the plain after an eruption. Freedom, the philosophic state par excellence, is synonymous with hardness.

Strangely enough—or rather, not so strangely—this coincides with *Vajrayana* Buddhism, which conceives of the wise man and the saint, the adept who has simultaneously attained wisdom and liberation, as a being made in the image and likeness of the diamond. *Vajrayana* is the "way" or doctrine of the bolt of lightning and the diamond. *Vajra* refers to a lightning bolt and also to the invulnerable, indestructible diamondlike nature both of the doctrine and of the state of beatitude that the ascetic attains to. At the same time *vajra* also stands for the male sex organ in Tantric rites and language. The vulva is the "house of *vajra*" and also wisdom. Series of metaphors composed of terms that now belong to the corporeal world, now to the incorporeal world: the lightning bolt and the phallus, the vulva and wisdom, the diamond and the beatitude of the liberated yogi. The series of material terms culminates in a metaphor that identifies the discharge of celestial fire with the hardness of the diamond—a petrification of the flame; the series of psychic terms ends with another image in which the carnal embrace is indistinguishable from the indifference of the ascetic during meditation—a transfiguration of passion into essence. The two metaphors in the end become one: a fusion of the macrocosm and the microcosm.

Pairs of contrasting concepts such as those I have just mentioned appear in all cultures. What seems significant to me is that in Tantric Buddhism the duality is manifested in this very fire/diamond, eroticism/indifference polarity. The final resolution of this double opposition in terms of the paired concepts diamond/indifference is no less notable. The supreme Buddha is *Vajrasattava*, the "adamantine essence" in Sanskrit; the Tibetans call him the "Lord of Stones." The surprising thing is that in its origin *vajra* (the lightning bolt) was the arm of Indra, the jolly, dissolute Vedic god. There is an arch that unites the two poles of the human spirit through the centuries. An arch which in this case goes from Indra, the god of storms and drunkenness, the god of the terrible burst of laughter that hurls all the elements into primordial confusion, to the impassible, imperturbable, adamantine Buddha, absorbed in the contemplation of his emptiness.

From the Vedic hymn to the manual on meditation, from the bolt of lightning to the diamond, from laughter to philosophy. The path from fire to stone, from passion to hardness, is analogous in the religious tradition of India and in European libertine philosophy. The difference is that the former offers us a total, though dizzying, vision of man and the world while the latter ends in a blind alley. In short, we live between the earthquake and petrification, between myth and philosophy. At one extreme, convulsive laughter pulls down the edifice of our principles and we run the risk of perishing beneath the ruins; at the other extreme, philosophy threatens us with mummification in life, whatever the mask we choose, whether it be that of Calvin or that of Sade. These are ruminations in the shadow of Coatlicue:[1] destruction through movement or through immobility. A theme for an Aztec moralist.

[1] An Aztec goddess represented with a girdle of skulls.

## INCARNATION AND DISSIPATION

Since man has been man, he has been exposed to aggression, either that of others or that of his own instincts. The expression "since man has been man" means, first, since our birth, and second, since the species stood up on its feet and adopted the erect posture. In this sense our condition is not historical: the dialectic of the pleasure principle and the reality principle unfolds in a zone untouched by the social changes of the last eight thousand years. Nevertheless, there is a difference: ancient societies established institutions and used methods that absorbed and transformed the aggressive instincts more easily and with less danger to the species than those of today. On one hand, systems of transformation of obsessions, impulses, and instincts into myths and collective images; on the other hand, rites: the incarnation of these images in ceremonies and festivals. I hardly need add that I believe neither in the superiority of those cultures that have preceded us nor in the superiority of our own culture. I fear that a "healthy society" is a utopia; and, if it is not, it is situated neither in the historical past nor in the future, at least the future such as we see it from the point of view of the present.[2] Nonetheless it seems obvious to me that antiquity (or antiquities, for there are several of them) offered a gamut of possibilities for sublimation and incarnation that was richer and more effective than ours.

So-called primitive cultures have created a system of meta-

[2] Claude Lévi-Strauss believes that if a golden age ever existed, it must have been in the villages of the Neolithic period. He may be right. The State was still in the embryonic stage, there was almost no division of labor, metals (arms) were unknown, as was writing (a bureaucracy of scribes/ a mass of slaves), and religion had not yet produced an organized clergy. Kostas Papaioannou told me almost the same thing a number of years ago, showing me little female fertility figures: happiness personified, a perfect accord with the world.

phors and symbols which, as Lévi-Strauss has shown, constitute a veritable code of signs that are both physical and intellectual: a language. The function of language is to point to meanings and communicate them, but we modern men have reduced the sign to its meaning, and communication to the transmission of information. We have forgotten that signs are physical things and work on the senses. Perfume transmits information that is inseparable from sensation. The same happens with taste, sound, and other sensory expressions and impressions. The rigor of the "logic of the senses" of primitive peoples amazes us by its intellectual precision, but the richness of their perceptions is no less extraordinary: where a modern nose distinguishes only a vague odor, a savage perceives a precise range of different smells. What is most astonishing is the method, the manner of associating all these signs, so that in the end they are woven into a series of symbolic objects: the world converted into a physical language. This is a double marvel: speaking with the body and converting language into a body.

Cyclic time is another way toward absorption, transformation, and sublimation. The date that recurs is a return of previous time, an immersion in a past which is at once that of each individual and that of the group. As the wheel of time revolves, it allows the society to recover buried, or repressed, psychic structures so as to reincorporate them in a present that is also a past. It is not only the return of the ancients and antiquity: it is the possibility that each individual possesses of recovering his living portion of the past. The purpose of psychoanalysis is to elucidate the forgotten incident, so that to a certain extent the cure is a recovery of memory. In ancient rites it is not memory that remembers the past but the past that returns. This is what I have called, in another context, the incarnation of images.

From this point of view, art is the modern equivalent of rites and festivals: the poet and the novelist construct symbolic objects, organisms that emit images. They do what the savage does: they convert language into a body. Though they do not cease to be signs, the words take on a body. Music also creates bodily languages, perceptible geometries. Unlike the poet and the musician, the painter and the sculptor make the body a language. Things become signs. The celebrated *Venus of the Mirror*, for example, is a variant of the sex/face metaphor. It is a response to Quevedo's verbal image and Posada's graphic metaphor: in Velázquez's painting, neither the face nor the genitals are humiliated. It is a moment of miraculous concord. The goddess—and there is nothing less celestial than this girl, lying stretched out on her own nudity, so to speak—turning her back on the spectator, as does Posada's dwarf. In the center of the painting, in the lower half, at the height at which we see dawn break, in the east, at precisely the place where the sun appears, is the perfect sphere of the girl's hips: a rump that is a celestial body. Above, in the upper horizon, at the zenith, in the center of the sky, is the face of the girl. Is it her face? More likely, as in the case of Góngora's Polyphemus, it is the reflection of it in the "neutral water" of a mirror. We are dizzied by it: the mirror reflects the face of an image, the reflection of a reflection; the crystallization of a moment which has already vanished in the real world.

Paintings: solitary rites of contemplation. Poems: a feast of phantoms, an invitation to watch reflections. Images take on flesh in art only to have it fall away in the act of reading or contemplating. What is more, the artist believes in art and not, like the primitive, in the reality of his visions. For Velázquez Venus is an image, for Góngora the solar eye of the Cyclops is a metaphor, and for Quevedo the Cyclopean anus is one more witty conceit. In all three cases there is something that does not belong to the realm of reality but to the realm of art. Poetic sublimation becomes more or less completely identical with the death instinct. At the same time, participation with others takes the form of reading. Primitive man also deciphers signs, he also reads, but his signs are a double of his body and the body of the world. The reading of primitive man is corporeal.

However mannered they may seem to us, Quevedo's conceit and Góngora's metaphor were still a living language. Though the seventeenth century may have forgotten that the body is a language, its poets managed to create a language that gives us the sensation of a living body—perhaps because it is so complicated. This body is not human: it is the body of Cyclopes and sirens, of centaurs and devils. A language that has suffered martyrdom and been possessed like a bewitched body. To measure the degree of abstraction and sublimation, we need only compare Quevedo's language with Swift's. Swift is a writer who is infinitely more free than the Spaniard, but his daring is almost exclusively intellectual. Swift would have been offended at Quevedo's sensual violence, especially on the scatological level. This is a matter not of morality but of taste: everything is permitted in the sphere of ideas and feelings, but not in that of sensibility. The eighteenth century, the libertine century, was also the inventor of good taste. Repression disappears in one zone only to appear in another, no longer wearing the mask of morality but the veil of aesthetics.

Swift's horror of female anatomy comes from Saint Augustine and it is echoed by two modern poets: William Butler Yeats and Juan Ramón Jiménez. In his best poem, "Espacio" ["Space"], Jiménez writes: "Love, love, love is *the place of excrement*," recalling Yeats's lines: "But Love has pitched his mansion in/The place of excrement." Although Quevedo probably felt the same sort of repulsion—he was a woman-hater, a whore-chaser, and a Petrarchist—his reaction is more wholehearted and, his pessimism notwithstanding, more healthy: "It [the eye of the ass as compared to the eyes of the face] is incomparably better, since in both men and women it is a close neighbor of the genital members; and this is a proof that it is better, according to the proverb that says: 'Tell me what sort of company you keep and I'll tell you who you are.' " In Quevedo's day the system of symbolic transformations of Catholicism still offers the possibility of speaking physically of physical things—even at a time when the Counter Reformation is beating a retreat and even though it takes the form of satire and scatology. In spite of the fact that Swift is freer intellectually than Quevedo, his sensuality encounters prohibitions no less powerful than those imposed on the Spanish poet by Neo-Scholasticism, absolute monarchy, and the Inquisition.

As repression becomes less rational, the inhibitions imposed upon sensual language increase. The extreme is Sade. No one has treated such inflammatory subjects in such cold and insipid language. His verbal ideal—when he does not give way to frenzy —is an erotic geometry and mathematics: bodies as ciphers and logical symbols, the love-positions as syllogisms. Abstraction borders on insensibility on one hand, and on boredom on the other. I do not want to disparage Sade's genius, even if the aura of veneration that has surrounded him for a number of years now makes me feel as though I am blaspheming against the great blasphemer. But there is nobody and nothing that can cause me to say that he is a sensual writer. The title of one of his works defines his language and his style: *Philosophy in the Bedroom*. The flame of passion is rekindled in the nineteenth century, and those who light it are the Romantic poets, who believed in true love and in the sublimity of the passions. The Romantic tide bears us on to Joyce and the Surrealists, a process that goes in the opposite direction from Sade and the eighteenth century: from the diamond to the bolt of lightning, from ataraxia to passion, from philosophy in the bedroom to poetry out of doors. And today another glacial era threatens us: the cold war is followed by cold libertinage. The debasement of forms is symptomatic of the lowering of erotic tension. The pleasure principle, which is explosion and subversion, is also, and above all, rite, representation; a festival, a ceremony. Sacrifice and courtliness: Eros is imaginary and cyclical, the exact opposite of the "happening," which occurs only once.

The phallus and the cunt are symbolic objects, and they are also sources of symbols. They are the body's language of passion, a language that only sickness and death—not philosophy—silence. The body is imaginary, not because it lacks reality, but because it is the most real reality: an image that is palpable yet ever-changing, and doomed to disappear. To dominate the body is to suppress the images it emits—and this domination is the purpose of the practices of the yogi and the ascetic. Or it is to make its reality disappear—and this is what the libertine does. Both practices aim at having done with the body, with its images and its nightmares: with its reality. For the reality of the body is a shifting image pinned down by desire. If language is the most perfect form of communication, the perfection of language cannot help but be erotic, and it includes death and silence: the failure of language. . . . Failure? Silence is not a failure, but the end result, the culmination of language. Why do we keep saying that death is absurd? What do we know about death?

Poetic metaphors and jokes express our dual reality. That the roots of the joke and those of art are the same has been said again and again since Freud wrote his famous essay on the subject. What people do not always remember is that this original similarity finally becomes opposition. Both the joke and the poem are expressions of the pleasure principle, which, for a moment, wins out over the reality principle. In both cases the triumph is imaginary; whereas the joke is transitory, in art there is a drive toward form. Is form a victory over death or a new trap of Thanatos? Perhaps it is neither. It is frenetic love, an exasperated and infinitely patient desire to freeze not the body but the movement of the body: the body moving toward death. The body jolted, driven by passion. I do not deny that art, like everything we do, is sublimation, culture, an homage to death. But it is a sublimation that seeks to incarnate: to return to the body. The joke is exemplary, and, whether it is cynical or satirical, it is moral. The ultimate morality lies in the fact that it is dissipated. Art is the opposite of dissipation, in the physical and spiritual sense of the word: it is concentration, desire that seeks incarnation.

# 2 | Conjugations

The pleasure principle is subversive. The ruling order, whatever it may be, is repressive: it is the order of domination. Social criticism frequently takes the form of a joke aimed at the pedantry of the educated and the ridiculous results of "good upbringing." It is an implicit—and at times explicit—tribute to the wisdom of the ignorant. Two systems of values confront each other: the culture of the poor and that of the rich. The first is inherited, unconscious, and ancient; the second is acquired, conscious, and modern. The opposition between the two is only a variation of the old dichotomy between nature and culture. It is Rousseau and Hobbes all over again: artificial society is authori-

[1] *"Un or néfaste incite pour son beau cadre une rixe . . ."* ("A malevolent gold prompts a quarrel for its handsome frame . . .") (Mallarmé, first version of the *Sonnet en ix*)

tarian and hierarchical; natural society is free and egalitarian. Sex is subversive not only because it is spontaneous and anarchical, but also because it is egalitarian: it has no name and no class. Above all, it has no face. It is not individual: it belongs to the species. The fact that sex has no face is the source of all the metaphors that I have mentioned, and also the source of our unhappiness. The sex organs and the face are separated, one below and one above; moreover, the former are hidden by clothes and the latter is uncovered. (Thus, covering the woman's face, as the Moslems do, is tantamount to affirming that she has no face: her face is a sex organ.) This separation, which has made us human beings, condemns us to labor, to history, and to the construction of tombs. It also condemns us to invent metaphors to do away with this separation. The sex organs and all their images—from the most complex down to jokes in a barroom—remind us that there was a time when our face was down close to the ground and to our genitals. There were no individuals and all human creatures were a part of the whole. The face finds this memory unbearable, and therefore it laughs —or vomits. Our sex organs tell us that there was a golden age; for the face, this age is not the solar ray of light of the Cyclops but excrement.

Max Weber discovered a relation between the Protestant ethic and the evolution of capitalism. Certain psychoanalysts, among them Erich Fromm, have stressed the connection between capitalism and anal eroticism. Norman O. Brown has brilliantly synthesized these two discoveries and has shown that the "excremental vision" constitutes the symbolic essence of modern civilization. The contradictory and complementary analogy between the sun and excrement is so evident that it almost needs no proof. It forms a pair of signs that alternately condense into one and become disassociated, ruled by the same syntax of symbols as other signs: fire and water, open and closed, pointed and round, wet and dry, light and shade. The rules of equivalence, opposition, and transformation that structural anthropology uses are perfectly applicable to these two signs, on either the individual level or the social level.

Anal eroticism is a pregenital phase of individual sexuality that corresponds to the golden age in the realm of social myths. There is little need to mention the infantile games and fantasies having to do with excrement. As for the mythic images: if the sun is life and death, excrement is death and life. The former gives us light and heat, but an excess of it kills us; it is life that can kill. The latter is refuse that is also a natural fertilizer: death that can give life. Excrement is the double of the phallus as the phallus is a double of the sun. Excrement is the *other* phallus, the *other* sun. It is sun that has rotted, as gold is congealed light: sun materialized in good solid ingots. Amassing gold is hoarding life (sun), and retaining excrement. Spending accumulated gold is disseminating life, transforming death into life. In the course of history all these images have become more and more abstract as instincts became more and more sublimated. The face drew farther and farther away from the ass.

The ambivalence of excrement and its identification with the sun and with gold gave it a sort of symbolic corporeality—sometimes beneficial and sometimes harmful—among primitive peoples as well as in antiquity and in the Middle Ages. Norman O. Brown is primarily interested in its recent metamorphoses. The associations and disassociations of gold and excrement constitute the secret history of modern society. The condemnation of excrement by the Reformation was the antecedent and the immediate cause of the capitalist sublimation: gold converted into banknotes and stock certificates. This transformation corresponds, on the level of symbols and beliefs, to the change, on the level of economy and day-to-day living, to the transition from a closed economy, based on things, to the open economy of the capitalist market, based on signs. Privies are the infernal place, by definition. The place where putrefaction occurs is the place where perdition occurs: this world. The condemnation of this world is the condemnation of putrefaction and of the passion for hoarding it and adoring it: the golden calf is excremental. This condemnation also has to do with waste. The connection between anal retention and a rational economy, which carefully calculates what is spent, is clear. Faced with choosing between hoarding and wasting, there was only one recourse: sublimation. The second step consisted in transforming this retention into a product: the hiding and sterilizing of the privy, and, at the same time, a metamorphosis of the cellar in which gold and riches were kept into the institution of the bank.

Even though the Protestant ethic dominated Mohammedans and Hindus for centuries, it failed to convert them. But it did manage to convert gold. It disappeared as a thing, lost its materiality and was transformed into a sign—and by a curious consequence of the Calvinist ethical system, into the sign of the elect. The miser is guilty of an infernal passion because he plays with the gold he hoards in his cellar as the child plays with its feces. The capitalist rational economy is useful and moral: it is the sacrifice by omission, the contrary of the sacrifice through waste and hecatomb. Divine recompense is not manifested in material goods but in signs: abstract money. At the same time that gold disappears from the dress of men and women and from altars and palaces, it becomes the invisible blood of mercantile society and circulates, odorless and colorless, in every country. It is not hoarded as in the Middle Ages, nor is it wasted and squandered: it circulates, it is created, it is counted and discounted, and thus it multiplies. It possesses a double virtue: it is both merchandise and a sign for all merchandise. The moralization of gold and its transmutation into a sign is parallel to the expulsion of dirty words from the language and to the invention and popularization of the English water closet. The bank and the toilet: typical expressions of capitalism.

Before Freud and his followers, Marx had already observed the magic character of gold in the civilization of antiquity. As for its relation with excrement, he said that capitalist society is "the domination of living men by dead matter." He should have added: the domination by *abstract* dead matter, since it is not material gold that asphyxiates us but rather the whole symbolic network that stands for it. In the countries that we call Socialist, more because this is a handy verbal label than because we are concerned about intellectual exactitude, individual profit has disappeared, and, consequently, the sign of gold has also disappeared. Nonetheless, power in these countries is not less but more abstract and stifling than in capitalist societies. The hidden connection between the anal aggressiveness and the abstract violence of the bureaucracies of the East should be studied. We would also have to determine what other infantile, pregenital erogenous zones this strange sublimation of the myth of the age of gold corresponds to, a sublimation that in reality is its negation. The transmutation of the primordial sun—the gold that was everybody's, when everything was gold—into the omniscient eye of the bureaucratic Police State is as impressive as the transformation of excrement into banknotes. But no one, so far as I know, has ever embarked upon an investigation of this subject. It is likewise a shame that none of us has ever examined from this point of view an artistic style which came into being precisely in the dawn of our era and which is the antithesis of both modern "socialism" and modern capitalism—a style that we might call "the excremental Baroque."

PYRES, MAUSOLEUMS, SANCTUARIES

The Counter Reformation, the "Jesuit style," and Spanish poetry of the seventeenth century are the other side of the coin of Protestant austerity and its condemnation and sublimation of excrement. Spain extracts gold from the Indies, at first from the altars of the devil (that is, from pre-Columbian temples) and later from the bowels of the earth. In both cases, it is a product of the lower world, the dominion of barbarians, Cyclopes, and the body. America is a sort of fabulous privy, except that now the operation does not consist in the retention of gold but in its dispersion. The dominant tone is not moral but mythical. The solar metal spreads over the fields of Europe in the form of senseless wars and mad undertakings, a proud excremental squandering of gold, blood, and passion: a monstrous, methodical orgy that is mindful of the ritual destructions of the American Indians, although much more costly. But the gold of the Indies also serves to cover the interiors of churches, like a solar offering. Altars and their golden vegetation of saints, martyrs, virgins, and angels blaze in the dark naves. They burn and slowly die. Gold more twilight than dawn because of the advancing shadow; a warm light and trembling reflections that evoke the ancient and ominous glories of the setting sun and excrement. Is this a life that brings on death or a death that brings on life? If gold and its physiological double are signs of the deepest and most instinctive tendencies of a society, they stand for just the opposite of productive accumulation in the Spanish and Hispano-American Baroque: they are profit that is sacrificed and burned up, the violent consumption of accumulated wealth. Rites of perdition and waste. Sacrifice and defecation.

The sun-excrement duality is polarized in the two great poets of the period, Góngora and Quevedo. The two of them are a sort of apotheosis of Spanish poetry: with them a great era of European literature comes to a close. I see their poems as a funeral ceremony, splendid burial rites of the sun-excrement. Although Góngora is the sun-poet, he does not hesitate to use the word shit when necessary; the most daring artist that poetry in the West has produced did not have what is called "good taste." There are also resplendent passages in Quevedo, the excremental poet. Speaking of a gold ring with the portrait of a woman inside it, he writes:

En breve cárcel traigo aprisionado
con toda su familia de oro ardiente,
el cerco de la luz resplandeciente . . .

[In a tiny cell I have imprisoned
with all its family of burning gold,
the halo of resplendent light . . .]

And farther on: "I have all the Indies in my hand." The gold of the New World and its infraterrestrial gleam as of a Cyclopean privy, but also the intellectual splendor of Neoplatonic eroticism: the beloved is light, the Idea. The Petrarchist heritage and the gold of the pre-Columbian idols, the medieval inferno and the glories of Flanders and Italy, the Christian heaven and the mythological firmament, with its stars, its flowers that "the great wild beasts with gleaming pelts" feed upon all glow in this etched flash of lightning. And that is why Quevedo also says, in another sonnet, without contradicting himself: "The voice of the eye, that we call a fart/the nightingale of male whores . . ." The anus as an eye that is also a mouth. All these images are possessed by the greed, the fury, and the glory of death. Their complexity and their obscenity have the grandeur of a ritual holocaust.

Excrement for Swift is a theme for moral meditation; for Quevedo it is a plastic material like rubies, pearls, and the Greek and Latin myths of the rhetoric of his age. Quevedo's pessimism is total: everything can be used to fan the flames. But this fire is a form, a style; the flames assume the shape of a verbal architecture and its sparks are intellectual: witticisms and conceits. Quevedo's example is not the only one. Throughout the Spanish Baroque period, both in the realm of poetry and that of the plastic arts, the opposition between gold and shadow, flame and darkness, blood and night reigns. These elements symbolize not so much the struggle between life and death as a mortal combat between two rival principles: this life and the other life, the world here and the world beyond, the body and the soul. The body tempts the soul; it seeks to consume it with passion so that it will hurl itself into the black pit. The soul, in turn, punishes the body; it punishes it with fire because it wishes to reduce it to ashes. The martyrdom of the flesh is somewhat the counterpart of the autos-da-fé and the burning of heretics. It is also the counterpart of the sufferings of the soul, crucified on the burning cross of the senses. In both cases, fire is purifying.

In this dialectic of light and shadow, of flame and smoldering coals, fire represents the same principle as the bolt of lightning in Tantric Buddhism: the transmutation, through meditation, of sexual passion into adamantine indifference corresponds to the transfiguration of flesh into spiritual light through fire in the Spain of the Counter Reformation. Another analogy: just as the ray of light (the phallus) must be transmuted into a diamond, so the tree (the human body) must be transformed into a cross. In both cases there is a reduction of the natural element (the ray of light, the tree) to its essential elements so as to change it into a sign (a cross and a stylized *vajra*). Martyrdoms and transfigurations of nature . . . But such is the power of passion, such is the body's capacity for pleasure, that the flames become a joy. Martyrdom does not extinguish pleasure—it heightens it. The contortions of the burning members hint at sensations in which delight and torture are intermingled. Not even the religious spirit was insensitive to the fascination of combustion. Our mystics' "I am dying because I am not dying" and their "pleasure at dying" are the opposite, the complement and the transfiguration, of the desperate "kill me's" and the "I am dying of pleasure's" of lovers. These are scorched souls and bodies. In our Baroque art the spirit vanquishes the body, but the body seizes upon the opportunity to glorify itself in the very act of dying. Its disaster is its monument.

The pleasure principle, even in these homages to death that Baroque poems are, always takes refuge in form. We are condemned to die, and thus sublimation inevitably serves the death instinct. Since we are also condemned to live, the pleasure principle erects immortal monuments (or would-be ones) to death. . . .

As I am writing this, I can see the mausoleums of the Lodi dynasty from my window—buildings the color of blood that is scarcely dry, cupolas blackened by the sun, the years, and the rains of the monsoon season, and others of marble, whiter than jasmin—and trees with fantastic foliage planted in meadows as geometric as syllogisms, and amid the silence of the pools and the blue enamel of the sky, the cawing of crows and the silent circling of birds of prey. A flock of parakeets, green streaks that appear and disappear in the quiet air like skyrockets, intersected by the dark wings of great bats. Some are returning to their nests to sleep; others have just awakened and fly drowsily. It is almost nightfall, and there is still a shadowy light. These tombs are not made of stone or gold: they are made of a lunar, vegetable material. Only the domes are visible now, great immobile magnolias. The sky dips down into the pool. There is no top or bottom: the world has been concentrated in this serene rectangle, a space which contains everything and is made up of nothing but air and a few fleeting images. The god of Islam is not my God, but it seems to me that the opposition between life and death is dissolved in these tombs. But not in Swift, not in Quevedo.

If we wish to find traces of the fusion of the face and the sex organs in the history of Spanish poetry, it is best to leave Góngora and Quevedo and seek another poet: Juan Ruiz, the "Archpriest of Hita." It will be said that I am forgetting, among others, Lope de Vega, Fernando de Rojas, and the great Francisco Delicado. I am not forgetting them. It is just that after the sumptuous and terrible ceremonies of gold, excrement, and death, I must go out and breathe the brisk and euphoric air of the fourteenth century. That is why I have sought out the universal clergyman in his little city. Perhaps he is off on one of his erotic hunting expeditions and is wandering about in the neighboring mountains, populated not by nymphs and centaurs, but by robust, licentious highland girls. Or he may be back in town, walking about in the atrium of the church, accompanied by Trotaconventos. The cleric and the bawd are weaving amorous nets or unraveling those that duennas and nuns have set out for them:

No me las enseñes más
que me matarás.
Estábase la monja
en el monesterio,
sus teticas blancas
de so el velo negro.
Más, que me matarás.[2]

[2] Diego Sánchez de Badajoz. (*Recopilación en metro*, 1554). Cited in *Lírica hispánica de tipo popular*, selección, prólogo y notas de Margit Frenk Alatorre (Mexico City, 1966).

[Don't show me any more
You'll kill me.
There the nun was
In the monastery,
Her white little breasts
Beneath the black veil.
No more, you'll kill me.]

In the *Libro de buen amor*, the book of passionate love, the scatology is not funereal, nor are the sex organs bloody and golden. There is neither exaggerated sublimation nor harsh realism, though the passions are most lively. There is not a trace of Platonism or of aristocratic hierarchies: the chatelaine is not an invulnerable castle, even though "she could not be swayed by any amount of money." This is great praise. The Archpriest really liked women; he knew that even though they are the dwelling place of death, they are also the banquet table of life. And this knowledge neither horrified him nor enraged him. No, we are not only descendants of Quevedo, nor in the case of us Mexicans, of the ascetic Quetzalcoatl and the ferocious Huitzilopochtli. We are also descendants of the Archpriest and his duennas and damsels, his Jewish and Moorish women—of them and of the naked girls of the Neolithic period, those little statues made of ears of dried corn unearthed in Tlaltilco, still intact and smiling at us.

Reading Quevedo in the garden of a fifteenth-century Moslem mausoleum may seem incongruous; but it is not incongruous to read the *Libro de buen amor* in these surroundings: its author lived among Moslems, many of whom, both men and women, were singers, dancers, and wandering minstrels. They are exactly like the ones who still wander about in Rajasthan or Uttar Pradesh, and sometimes, when they pass through New Delhi, they sit in a circle in the meadows surrounding the mausoleums, eating, sleeping, or singing. The historic closeness of Spain and Islam does not blot out the obvious and vast differences between the mausoleum and the book of the Spanish poet. At the moment, what I should like to emphasize is this: the mausoleum reconciles life with death, and thus it is the latter that wins out; the book joins death and life, and what wins out is life. In both cases there is a dialogue between the two principles. It is not right, of course, to compare a book to a monument. What, then, is the Western counterpart of these tombs? I cannot really answer that question. I have never felt this lightness of touch and this serenity in any Christian cemetery. The cemeteries of the Greeks and Romans? Perhaps—except they do not seem to me to be as airy and as welcoming as these mausoleums. History weighs heavily there; here it disappears: it is a story, a legend. The answer lies outside of Europe and monotheism—here again in India, in the Hindu temples and the Buddhist chaityas. They are not tombs: the Indians burn their dead. Yet many of these sanctuaries contain bones of saints and even teeth and other relics of Buddha. In Indian temples life does not fight death: it absorbs it. And life, too, melts away—as a day melts away into the year and a year into a century.

In Indian sanctuaries, existence is conceived as proliferation and manifests itself with an insistent, monotonous richness that is mindful of the irregularity and the persistence of wild vegetation; in Moslem mausoleums nature is submitted to a geometry that is at once implacable and elegant: circles, rectangles, hexagons. Even water is transformed into geometry. Imprisoned in canals and pools, it is laid out in geometric spaces: it is a vision; it falls on a stone fountain or murmurs between marble banks; it is divided into regular units of time: it is sound. It is a play of echoes and correspondences between time and space; the eye, delighted by the harmonic divisions of space, contemplates the reflection of the stone in the water; the ear, entranced by the repetition of the same rhyme, listens to the sound of the water falling on the stone. The difference between the Indian temple and the Moslem mausoleum is a radical one; on the one hand, we are in the presence of a monism that includes the pluralism of the natural world, and a very rich and complicated polytheism; on the other, we are in the presence of an intransigent monotheism that excludes any sort of natural plurality or even the slighest trace of polytheism. In Indian civilization there is an exaltation of the body; in Islam the body disappears in the geometry of stone and garden.

When we speak of the temples of India we must make a distinction between Hindu and Buddhist sanctuaries. Inside India, Hinduism and Buddhism were the protagonists of a dialogue. This dialogue was Indian civilization. The fact that it has now ended helps explain the prostration of this civilization for over eight centuries, and its inability to renew itself and change. The dialogue degenerated into the monologue of Hinduism, a monologue that soon assumed the form of repetition and mannerism until, finally, ossification set in. Islam, appearing just as Buddhism disappears in India, failed to take its place: the opposition between Hinduism and Buddhism is a contradiction within one and the same system, whereas that between Islamism and Hinduism is the confrontation of two different and incompatible systems. Something similar occurred later in the case of Christianity and, today, is occurring with the ideologies linked to this religion: democracy, socialism . . . The West has experienced nothing similar to an intrusion of a completely different religion; the non-Christian religions it confronted were versions of the same monotheism: Judaism and Islamism.

The orientalists and philosophers who have described Buddhism as a nihilism that denies life were blind: they never saw the sculptures at Bharhut, Sanchi, Muttra, and other similar places. If Buddhism is pessimistic—and I do not see how a critical system of thought can fail to be—its pessimism is radical and includes the negation of the negation: it denies death with the same logic with which it denies life. In the period when Buddhism flourished, this dialectical refinement allowed it to accept and glorify the body. But in the great Hindu temples of Khajuraho and even in Konarak—which is less rococo and really imposing in its beautiful vastness—eroticism reaches the point of being monotonous. Something is missing: happiness or death, a spark of real passion to animate the interminable garlands of undulating bodies and faces that smile in a sort of sugary beatitude. Ecstasy here is mass-produced, a mannered orgasm. Nor is nature present in these corporeal games, which are more complicated than impassioned. Hinduism is excessive not so much because of its intrinsic powers, which are considerable, as because it has digested all its heterodoxies and contradictions; its excessive affirmation lacks the counterweight of negativity—that critical element that is the creative nucleus of Buddhism. Thanks to the Buddhist negation, ancient India changed, transformed itself, and re-created itself; once its negation was extirpated or assimilated, India did not grow: it proliferated. Its eroticism became superficial, epidermal: a tissue of sensations and contractions.

The entwined bodies of Khajuraho are like those commentaries of a commentary of a commentary of the *Brahma Sutra*: the subtleties of the argument do not always add up to real profundity, which is simple. The pullulation of breasts, phalluses, haunches, muscles, and ecstatic smiles are, ultimately, cloying. This is not true in the Buddhist monuments, not in Bharhut and above all not in Karli. The great reliefs sculptured in the face of the portals of Karli are naked, smiling couples, not goddesses or demons but beings like ourselves, although stronger and livelier. The radiant health of their bodies is natural, with the somewhat heavy solidity of mountains and the slow grace of broad rivers. They are natural, civilized beings: there is immense courtesy in their powerful sensuality and their passion is peaceful. They are planted there like trees— except that they are trees that smile. No other civilization has created such complete and such perfect images of earthly joy. For the first and only time a high historical culture was able to rival the Neolithic and its little fertility figures, and not come off the worse from the comparison—the opposite pole from Islam and its geometry of reflections at the bottom of pools.

## CONJUGATIONS

Capitalism and Protestantism, the Counter Reformation and Spanish poetry, Moslem mausoleums and Indian temples: why is it that no one has ever written a general history of the relations between the body and the soul, life and death, the sex organs and the face? Doubtless for the same reason that no one has written a history of man. We have, instead, histories of men, that is to say, of civilizations and cultures. This is not surprising: to date no one knows what "human nature" really is. And we do not know because our "nature" is inseparable from culture, and culture is cultures. For this reason the American anthropologist A. L. Kroeber has suggested a two-pronged investigation: first, making a universal inventory of the characteristic traits—material, institutional, and symbolic—of the different cultures and civilizations, traits aimed at "determining the perimeters of human culture"; and, second, making another inventory "among the subhuman animals, of forms of conduct that are similar or anticipatory of human cultural forms."[3] Using this catalogue as a base, we could begin to construct both a theory of culture and a theory of human nature. It may be that at the end of this task, which reminds me of that of Sisyphus, we will manage to situate, if not to define, our nature. It is obvious that it is to be found at the point of intersection between human culture and the animal subculture: but where is this point?

For the moment we can merely repeat that soul and body, face and sex organs, life and death are different realities that have different names in each civilization, and, therefore, different meanings. This is not all: it is impossible to translate the central terms of one culture into those of another: *mukti* is not really liberation, nor is *nirvana* extinction. The same thing happens with the *tê* of the Chinese, the *dēmokratia* of the Greeks, the *virtus* of the Romans, and the *yugên* of the Japanese. When we seem to be speaking of the same things with an Arab or an Eskimo, we may be speaking of different things; and it is not inconceivable that the opposite might also be true. But even though we cannot reduce the different meanings of all these terms to a single univocal pattern, we at least know that they are somewhat analogous. We likewise know that they constitute the common preoccupation of all men and of all societies. The moment we examine this difficulty carefully, we see that we are faced not so much with a diversity of realities as a plurality of meanings. The objection may fairly be raised that if we do not know for certain what a word means, we will have even less of an idea of what reality is being referred to. This is true, but the criticism also applies just as much to our terms as to those of another culture: for us, too, the words life, soul, and body are

---

[3] Alfred L. Kroeber, *An Anthropologist Looks at History: Selected Essays* (Berkeley, 1963).

changing words with changing meanings designating changing realities. If we accept the advice of the modern philosophy of language, we ought to follow it to the very end: what it advises us to do is shut our mouths and not say a single word. This may be the most rational thing to do, but not the wisest. So without denigrating logicians, I shall proceed. . . .

Each of the words that we are here concerned with possesses, within its own linguistic area, more or less definite relationships with the others: life with death, sex with spirit, body with soul. These relationships are not always bilateral: they may also be triangular, even circular. There is a biopsychic circuit that goes from life to sex to spirit to death to life. Nonetheless, the basic relationship is that between pairs. Whatever the particular meaning of the terms that compose it, this relationship is universal: it exists everywhere and it has almost surely existed throughout human history. There is another factor that is no less decisive and determining: in each instance we are faced not with realities but with names. In view of all this, it is not going too far to believe that we may some day construct a universal syntax of civilizations, such as the one Lévi-Strauss and his school are constructing for primitive societies. I should like to point out that this syntax could be constructed even though we are as yet unable to study the semantic aspect in depth. We must first find out how the signs function, how they are interrelated, and then determine what they mean. This investigation would attack the problem from a perspective diametrically opposed to that suggested by Kroeber. The combination of these two investigations would be the point of departure for a true history of man.

Basically, the relationship between the terms can only be one of opposition or of affinity. Too much opposition cancels out one of the terms of which it is composed; too much affinity also destroys it. Thus the relationship is always threatened, either by an excessive conjunction or by a disjunction that also is excessive. The predominance of one of the terms disturbs the balance; absolute equality between the two terms produces neutralization, and, as a consequence, immobility. The ideal relationship demands a certain slight disequilibrium of forces and a relative autonomy of each term with respect to the other. This slight disequilibrium implies on the one hand a recourse to sublimation (culture) and on the other hand the possibility of injecting spontaneity into the culture (creation); and this limited autonomy is called freedom. The essential thing is for the relationship not to be a tranquil one: the dialogue between oscillation and immobility is what gives a culture life and life form. There is another condition, governed like the preceding ones by the rules that structural anthropology has discovered: the terms are not intelligible except in relation to each other; they cannot be understood if they are studied one by one. This is something that Chuang-tzu said long ago: the word life has meaning only when compared to the word death, the word heat when compared to the word cold, the word dry when compared to wet. Finally, since it is impossible to translate the terms that compose the relation in each civilization (soul/body, spirit/nature, *purusa/ prakṛti*, etc.), the best thing to do would be to use two signs from logic or algebra which would include them all. Or we might use the words *body* and *non-body*, providing it is understood that they have no meaning except to express a contradictory relation. *Non-body* means neither *ātman* nor *tê* nor *psyche*; it is simply the contrary of *body*. And *body* in turn has no special connotation: it simply denotes the contrary of *non-body*.

It seems to me that if these observations were pursued further and systematically formulated, a method of investigation based on them, applicable both to the study of societies and to that of individuals, might be worked out. I say individuals and not only societies because the signs *body* and *non-body* either conflict with each other or are reunited, both in individuals and in their work, as we have seen in the case of Velázquez and Posada. My proposition, let me add, is a very modest one; I am suggesting something less than a syntax or a morphology of cultures: a thermometer, a very simple instrument to measure the degrees of cold or heat of a mind and of a civilization. The temperature chart of a society over a rather long period of time is not the same, of course, as its history, but the curves upward or downward are a precious index of its vitality, its resistance, and its ability to face other ups and downs. The comparison of the temperature charts of different civilizations can teach us, or rather confirm, what we all know empirically: that there are cold civilizations, warm civilizations, and others in which there are sudden alternations of periods of chills and periods of fever. And how do civilizations die? Some of them, the cold ones, die of a sudden combustion; the warm ones die by a slow cooling process that produces first desiccation and then pulverization; others, which are overly secluded, perish the moment they are exposed to storms; and others sleep for whole millennia in the gentle warmth of a normal temperature or commit suicide in a delirium brought on by fever.

The relations between the signs that orient the life of civilizations have often been studied, although never in an explicit and systematic manner. We hardly need recall the work of Georges Dumézil on the Indo-Europeans and what he calls their "tripartite ideology." This is a hypothesis that is as daring as it is fruitful and one that opens a new path not only for studies of Indo-European mythology but also for studies of different civilizations. Perhaps some day someone will dare to study the civilizations of the Far East (China, Korea, Japan) and pre-Columbian America from Dumézil's point of view. It is not inconceivable that such a study would verify what many of us suspect: that the tendency of both civilizations to think in quadripartite terms is something more than a mere coincidence.

Perhaps duality, thinking in terms of pairs, is common to all men, and what distinguishes civilizations is the manner in which they combine the basic paired terms: in tripartite, quadripartite, or circular structures.

Another example, taken this time from within a definite historical period, is Huizinga's classic study on the waning of the Middle Ages. The Dutch historian describes the stormy relations between the pleasure principle and the death instinct, the repressions of the latter and the rebellions of the former, the function of waste and holocaust in tourneys, the eroticism, the avarice, and the prodigality of princes, and the incarnation of all these contradictory tensions in the antithetical figures of Louis XI and Charles the Bold. The alternate domination of each of these principles (signs) in the course of the history of a civilization might also be studied. This has already been done several times, and done brilliantly. One of the favorite areas of exploration is the contrast in the West between the exalted spiritual tone of the twelfth and thirteenth centuries and the sensual coloration of the Renaissance. And we owe to E. R. Dodds a masterful description of the progressive, asphyxiating domination of the concept of the *soul* on ancient Greek beliefs up until the time when the rebellion of the *body* rent the fabric of the Greek social ethic.[4] Dodds has also published another book, *Pagan and Christian in an Age of Anxiety* (London, 1965), which can be considered the complement of his previous book. In it he has undertaken the study of the period from Marcus Aurelius to Constantine. In his first book, he describes the rebellion of the irrational (the *body*) against the rigors of classical philosophy and its rational constructs; in the second, he examines the anguished irrational substratum of the twilight of ancient civilization and the transformation of these impulses into a new

[4] *The Greeks and the Irrational* (London, 1951).

religious rationality (the *non-body*). Dodds's books are something more than that, of course, but what I wish to emphasize is the decisive role played by the signs that I have called the *body* and the *non-body*.

The comparison between different civilizations has been the province where Toynbee has reigned, or did until very recently. Before that it was the domain of Spengler, who has today been discredited, and not always with good reason. Among recent studies of this type there is one by Jacques Soustelle, *Les quatre soleils* (Paris, 1967), in which the French anthropologist offers a series of reflections on the possible fate of Western civilization. The most notable feature of the book is that the author views the future from the perspective of the cosmogonic conceptions of the ancient Mayas and Mexicans. I believe that this is the first time that anyone has contemplated universal history from the vantage point of Meso-American civilization. Soustelle points out the surprising modernity of pre-Columbian thought. I want to emphasize that this cosmogony in perpetual rotation, based on the alternate pre-eminence of the creative principle and the destructive principle, reveals a pessimism and a wisdom no less profound than Freud's. It is yet another example, and perhaps the clearest one, of the dynamic relation between the signs *body* and *non-body*. I might draw another analogy: in the Meso-American philosophy of movement, the notion of a cosmic catastrophe—the end of each "sun," or era, by a cataclysm—is equivalent to our modern notion of an Accident, both in the sciences and in our life in history. Another feature that brings the Meso-Americans even closer to us is the excessive increase of aggressive instincts in the final phase of this civilization. The sadism of the Aztec religion and its sexual puritanism, the institution of the "florid war," and the rigorous nature of Tenochca political conceptions are expressions of an exaggerated disjunction between the signs *body* and *non-body*. They correspond to our idea of technology as a will-to-power, to the high water-mark of militant ideologies, to the puritanism of the countries of Eastern Europe, and to their counterpart, the cold and no less fanatic promiscuity of the West, and, finally, to the warlike spirit of all our enterprises, including those that are apparently most peaceful. Aesthetics itself is military in our culture: a matter of avant-gardes, advances, breaks, conquests. The parallel with Náhuatl art is surprising: the symbolic system of Aztec poetry—its metaphors, its similes, its vocabulary—was a sort of verbal double of the "florid war," which, in turn, was the double of cosmic war. The same analogical system governed sacred architecture, sculpture, and the other arts; they were all representations of universal movement: the war of the gods, of the stars, of men.

All these examples reveal that there is a sort of combinatory system governing the basic signs of each civilization and that the character of each society, including its future, depends on the relationship between these signs. Later I will attempt to show, in a more concrete and systematic manner, the forms—or rather some forms—whereby the signs unite and separate. In no case does the relationship disappear, however pronounced the disjunction or the conjunction. The association of signs, whether it be strong or weak, is what distinguishes us humans from the other animals. Rather, it is what makes us complex, problematical, and unpredictable beings. Since the dialectic of opposition and fusion unfolds within all men in all periods of history, I shall use the comparative method. I shall use examples taken from the West, from India, and from China, since I believe that Indian civilization is the other pole of that of the West, the other version of the Indo-European world. The relationship between India and the West is that of an opposition within a system. The relationship of both with the Far East (China, Japan, Korea, and Tibet) is a relationship between two different systems. Chinese examples in these reflections are thus neither convergent nor divergent: they are excentric. (What is the other pole of the world of China and Japan? Perhaps it is pre-Columbian America.) Finally, it would be insulting the reader's good sense if I were to warn him that I am not attempting to reduce history to a combination of signs such as those of the *I Ching* hexagrams. Signs, whether those from heaven or those of modern science, do not foretell our destiny: nothing is written in advance.

# 3 | Eve and Prajnaparamita

## THE YAKSHI AND THE VIRGIN

Whatever the word and the particular meaning of *body* and *non-body* within each civilization, the relationship between these two signs is not, and cannot be, anything but unstable. Although the relationship is unsteady and precarious, there are a few rare moments of dynamic equilibrium. These moments are not a time of truce but a time for contradictory and creative dialogue. I have mentioned Indian Buddhist art, which goes from Bharhut and Sanchi to Muttra, Karli, and Amaravati; a parallel example in the West would be the art of the Middle Ages, from the Romanesque to Gothic. In Buddhist art the accent is placed on the corporeal, out of complementary opposition to the critical intellectualism and the ascetic rigor of Buddhism; in the face of medieval Catholicism—which is more corporeal and less radical in its criticism of the world and of existence—the figures

of virgins and saints express the spiritual and incorporeal element, through the workings of the same law of complementary
opposition. The representative male and female fertility figures
(*yaksa* and *yaksī*) and the erotic couples (*maithuna*) that cover
the exterior parts of the chaityas surround the very sanctuary of
emptiness: a disincarnated man, the Buddha; the virgins, saints,
and angels of the medieval churches and cathedrals surround
an incarnated god, Christ. The extreme of disincarnation is the
portrayal of Buddha by his aniconic symbols: the stupa, the
tree of illumination, the throne, the wheel of doctrine; the response to this abstraction is the vitality and the sensuality of
the sculptures of the yakshis. The extreme of incarnation is the
representation of the birth of Christ and the episodes of his life
on earth, above all that of his passion and sacrifice; the response
to the blood and the martyred body of the god is the ascent into
heaven and the transfiguration of the body.

The great period of Buddhist art coincides with the appearance, around the first century A.D., of the first Prajnaparamita
Sutra, the origin of the madhyamika tendency. This doctrine
preaches a radical relativism which eventually brings it to the
point of maintaining that absolute emptiness (*śūnyatā*) is the
only reality. Since everything is relative, everything participates
in absolute nonreality, everything is empty; and therefore a
bridge is constructed between the phenomenal world (*saṁsāra*)
and emptiness, between the reality of this world and its unreality. Reality and unreality are terms that are relative, inter-
dependent, and opposed; at the same time they are identical.
The art of the Middle Ages, in turn, is contemporary with
Scholasticism, which delves into and refines the Aristotelian
notion of degrees of being, as expressed in the moderate realism
of Saint Thomas Aquinas. Thus the two religions postulate the
existence of various levels of ontological reality, the first moving
in the direction of emptiness and the second in the direction of

a fullness of being. These levels are degrees, or mediations, be-tween the corporeal and the spiritual, the pleasure principle and the death instinct. In this way they open up a whole gamut of possibilities for combining the contradictory signs. Both in Buddhist sanctuaries and in Christian cathedrals grotesque mon-sters and licentious and comic representations appear side by side with images of Buddha or Christ and their symbols. Be-tween the lower world and the upper world there is a gradation of modes of being—or of modes of emptiness. In both cases the equilibrium is based on a slight disequilibrium: corporeality and sensuality in Buddhism, and spiritual transfiguration of bodies in medieval Catholicism. A religion that denies the reality of the body exalts it in its most striking form, eroticism; but a religion that has made incarnation its central dogma spiritualizes and transfigures the flesh.

The divergent evolution of these two movements—the dia-lectic inherent in the contradictory relation between the signs *body* and *non-body*—can be clearly seen in both religions. Buddhism is born in nonpriestly and aristocratic surroundings: Gautama belonged to the royal clan of the sakya and hence was a member of a warrior caste; his preaching from the start was well received by the nobles and above all by merchants, so that it soon became a religion of renunciation practiced by an urban, cosmopolitan, and well-to-do class; in its ultimate Indian expression, Tantrism, it is transformed into a religion of wan-dering mystics outside of society, and flourishes in the lower castes. Christianity is born in priestly and proletarian surround-ings: Jesus is the son of a carpenter and a descendant of the House of David; the first Christians belong to the world that lives on the social periphery of the Roman Empire; later, Chris-tianity was the official religion of an empire and, later still, it adopted an imperial organization itself; in its final form, Prot-estantism, it became the ascetic religion of capitalism.

Christianity ends where Buddhism begins. This latter, when it first began its career as a universal religion, was just one sect more among those that had undertaken to criticize the Brahmanical religion and reconsider the tradition of the Upanishads in the sixth century B.C. In this context the figures of Gautama, Mahavira, and other religious reformers recall the theologians of the first days of the Reformation—Luther, Zwingli, and Calvin. But in the course of its history, Buddhism wanders further and further away from its original critical and moral tendencies and progressively stresses its ritual and metaphysical features: the Mahayana philosophical systems, the cult of the image of Buddha, the appearance of Bodhisattvas as saviors of men, the doctrine of the universal compassion of the Buddhas, the increasing formality and complexity of Buddhist ritual and ceremony. The steps were: a criticism of the traditional religion; a religious philosophy; a metaphysical religion; a ritualistic religion. A contrary evolution can be observed in the case of Christianity: it is born as a doctrine of salvation and an announcement of the end of the world, that is to say, as a real religion and not only as a criticism or a reform of Judaism; it confronts pagan thought and creates a philosophy thanks to the Church Fathers; it constructs a great metaphysical system in the Middle Ages; it passes during the Reformation from metaphysics to criticism and from ritual to ethics. Analogous movements but in opposite directions: in Buddhism, from criticism and ethics to metaphysics and liturgy; in Christianity from metaphysics to ethics, and in the ritual sphere, a fading away of the notion of the eucharist, and the supremacy of the evangelical word (ethics) over the divine presence (the sacrament). Incarnation and disincarnation.

The evolution of artistic styles does not seem initially to display the same correspondence. Nevertheless, if the visual field is marked off with a fair degree of precision, the reverse-image symmetry appears once again, although not with the same clarity as it does in the evolution of these two religions. The first difficulty is that neither Christian art nor Buddhist art coincides, respectively, with the spatial and temporal limits of Western or Indian civilization. The area of comparison must therefore be carefully defined: in one case we must consider the Christian art of the West, excluding the art of primitive Christianity (the Greco-Roman appendage), and Byzantine, Coptic, and Syrian art; in the other case, we must consider Indian Buddhist and Hindu art, excluding the art of China, Korea, and Japan, though not the art of Nepal, Ceylon, Java, Cambodia, and Burma, which from the point of view of artistic styles are part of Indian civilization. (Tibet occupies an intermediate place that is a case in itself.) The second obstacle standing in the way of comparison is the different evolution of the two civilizations. We must again set limits: does the Vedic world represent what Greco-Roman civilization represents for the West, or is it simply the first period of Indian civilization? However we answer this question, it is clear that around the sixth century B.C. something new begins in India—either a distinct phase of Vedic civilization or a new civilization.[1]

Kroeber distinguishes two phases in Western civilization: medieval Catholic and modern. The high point reached in the

[1] The connection between the civilization of the Indus and that of India is doubtful, to say the least. Apart from the fact that they are separated by a millennium or more, that of the Indus appears to be more akin to the Mesopotamian world, and, specifically, to the Sumerian-Babylonian world. Nonetheless, there appear to be certain features in Hinduism that may have come from Mohenjo-daro and Harappa, such as the cult of Siva and the Great Goddess. There are some scholars who believe that yoga practices and the caste system have the same pre-Aryan origin.

late Middle Ages was followed by a period of disruption and confusion, which was followed by a revolutionary recombination of the elements of our civilization, a new period: the period in which we are still living and which, it appears, is coming to an end. In the West there occurred what Kroeber calls "a reconstitution within civilizations." There are differences between the Newtonian universe and the Einsteinian, but they are the same universe; the universe of Saint Thomas and Abelard is another universe, different from ours. India from the sixth century B.C. to the thirteenth century experienced nothing similar to the Renaissance, the Reformation, the Enlightenment, and the Industrial Revolution. There was no "reconstitution," only repetition, mannerism, self-imitation, and, finally, sclerosis. It was not the invasions of white Huns that put an end to Indian civilization but that civilization's inability to reconstruct itself or fecundate itself.

Two facts perhaps explain the slow petrification of India and its final crumbling in its Middle Ages: first, its Reformation (Buddhism) took place at the beginning of Indian civilization; second, the triumph of the Hindu Counter Reformation dislodged the merchant classes, the patrons of Buddhism, from the center of social life and put the local warlords and Brahmins in their place when the empire of the Guptas collapsed. This latter turn of events represented the end of the central monarchy and, therefore, of a Pan-Indian state: a consolidation of feudalism and the caste system. Indian civilization ended in what the historians call the Hindu Middle Ages. It can thus be said that in its main outline Indian history is a process that is the reverse image of what happened in the West. . . . Therefore, in order for the comparison to make sense, it must deal with the first phase of Western civilization (medieval Catholicism) and Indian civilization from the sixth century B.C. onward. The disparity of time does not matter: what happened over a period of approximately two thousand years in India happened in less than a thousand years in the West.

The historians distinguish four periods in the art of the West: the formative, the Romanesque, the Gothic, and the flamboyant Gothic. The division of Indian art into periods is more uncertain and the vocabulary even vaguer. In general, three stages are mentioned: Buddhist, the Gupta and post-Gupta, and the Hindu medieval. The Buddhist period also can be, and should be, divided into two periods, both from the point of view of their duration and from the point of view of their stylistic changes: a formative period, not without certain resemblances with that of the West, which reaches its most perfect expression in the balustrades of the stupa of Bharhut; and another period at the zenith: Muttra, Sanchi (the toranas of the great stupa), Amaravati, Nagarjunanikonda, and Karli. The early period is preceded by a stage in which primitive Buddhism does not possess what can properly be called an artistic style; the flamboyant Gothic, the last stage in the West, is followed by a stylistic change that is a total break (the Renaissance) with medieval Christianity and a religious movement that does not even possess a style of its own: the Reformation.

The reliefs of Bharhut are the first great work of Indian art. The style of a whole civilization is born with these admirable sculptures, a style that neither historical and religious changes nor foreign influences—such as that of Gandhara—will modify in any substantial way and which will last until the thirteenth and fourteenth centuries. Before Bharhut there is nothing that merits the name of a style: neither the stupas that come from the Vedic period nor the cosmopolitan art of the Maurya dynasty. The formative period of the art of the West also emerges from a zone that is vague as far as style is concerned: the influences of the barbarians, the Byzantines, and the Greco-Roman past. Carolingian art is an abortive attempt to resurrect an imperial style; that of the Mauryas is another abortive attempt to adopt a foreign imperial style.[2] The art of the West and that of India in their formative periods are as much a reaction against the two false universalisms that precede them (Carolingian art and the Greco-Persian cosmopolitanism of the Mauryas) as they are a transformation of the heritage that was more rightly theirs: in the one case the Greco-Roman past and the art of the barbarians, and in the other case, the Vedic stupa. These are two styles in search of themselves, which find themselves, respectively, in Cluny and in Bharhut. These external similarities make the spiritual oppositions of meaning and orientation more revealing. In Bharhut the balustrade around the aniconic symbol of the Disincarnated is a deliberate exaltation of sensual and profane life. The separation is absolute, but the representation of scenes in the previous lives of the Buddha (*jātakas*) constructs a bridge between the attributes of the sign *body* and the absence of attributes of the sign *non-body*. Byzantine art had so highly stylized the divine presence that it becomes an atemporal symbol; the arts of the barbarians also tended toward abstraction and ornamentation; in both tendencies the sign takes precedence over the human figure, line over volume; this is antisculptural art. Medieval Christian art reinvents the art of sculpture, which is first and foremost the representation of the sacred figure: the body of

[2] Ananda K. Coomaraswamy maintains that there is no such Persian influence and that the pillars and capitals of Asoka are proof of a general relation to the art of Western Asia, especially Babylon and Assyria, rather than to that of Persepolis. To my mind, everything seems to indicate the contrary: the intimate relations of the Mauryas with the Seleucids; the presence of Persian and Greek artisans in Pataliputra, the capital of the Indian Empire; and, above all, the polish and high degree of perfection of these pillars and of the animal figures that crown the capitals, in the best tradition of the hybrid, official, and imperial art of the court of the Great King and his Greek successors.

the incarnated God. The first great work of Romanesque sculpture is perhaps the tympanum of the portal of Saint-Pierre de Moissac. It is a representation of the Last Judgment: the figure of the Lord—hieratic, radiant, immense—surrounded by tiny animated figures. The contrast is significant: in Bharhut Nothingness is god and everything adores it; in Saint-Pierre de Moissac Being is god and reigns over all.

The following two stages are the apogee of Buddhist art in India and mature Romanesque in the West. I have already mentioned the earthly sensuality of the yakshis of Karli, Muttra, and Sanchi; I now want to point to the vitality of Romanesque sculpture, which is sometimes demoniacal and sometimes divine. Either we find the body in its most elemental, sensual, and direct expression, or we find the body traversed by other-worldly forces and impulses that are not corporeal. The dissolution of reality is the counterpart in Buddhism of the resurrection of the flesh in Christianity. It is in this era that Buddha ceases to be represented only by his symbols and comes to be represented as a presence. This change is one of the consequences of the great religious revolution that Buddhism undergoes: the Prajnaparamita Sutras proclaim the doctrine of the Bodhisattvas; a little later, Nagarjuna and his followers elaborate and refine the notion of sunyata. Through the first of these developments an affective element is introduced into the austere Buddhist rigor: the figures of the Bodhisattvas who, moved by compassion, renounce Buddhism, or rather, transcend it: their mission is to save all living beings.[3] Through the second of these develop-

[3] The ideal of Hinayana Buddhism is the Arhant, the ascetic who reaches nirvana through concentration and meditation and abandons the phenomenological world (*saṁsāra*); Mahayana Buddhism exalts the figure of the Bodhisattva, in whom "perfect wisdom" unites with compassion; in its final form (*Vajrayāna*), Tantric Buddhism accentuates the passional element of Compassion. When I refer to Tantrism I shall write (com)Passion, although the Sanskrit word is the same: *karuṇā*.

ments, Buddhism regains the world, thanks to the radical relativism of Nagarjuna. The bridge between existence and extinction ceases to be a bridge; nothingness is identical with phenomenal reality, and perceiving its identity and realizing it is to leap to the other shore, to attain "perfect wisdom" (*prajñā-pāramitā*). Romanesque art links the ideas of order and rhythm. It conceives of the church as a space that is the sphere of the supernatural. But it is a space on this earth: the church does not seek to escape the earth; rather, it is the place where Presence manifests itself, a place laid out by reason and measured by rhythm. The old Greek and Mediterranean spirit, with its fondness for both the human form and for geometry, is still there, but it is now expressed in a new language. In India, a strict and devastating rationality breaks through the limits between phenomenal reality and the absolute and recovers the sign *body*, which ceases to be the opposite of *non-body*. In the West reason traces the limits of the sacred space and constructs churches in the image of absolute perfection: it is the earthly dwelling place of the *non-body*. These are the two great moments of Buddhism and Christianity and in both a dynamic equilibrium, a plenitude is achieved, if not an impossible harmony between the two signs.

Gupta and post-Gupta art are the reverse image of the Gothic. The first difference is that the Gupta and post-Gupta period is, above all, the period of a Hindu Renaissance—especially as regards the cult of Vishnu. The great innovation in architecture is the invention of the prototype of the Hindu temple; Buddhist sculpture in this period is less interesting,[4] and the same must be said for architecture and painting (the late frescoes of Ajanta give us some idea of what this latter must have been like). Unlike what happens in the West, one and the same artistic style serves to express different religious tendencies

[4] See *India*, by Hermann Goetz, Art of the World Series (London, 1959).

and institutions: Hinduism, Buddhism, Jainism. The same thing had happened before, except that in the first two periods Indian art was essentially Buddhistic, whereas in this period Buddhism not only coexists with Hinduism but in the end yields up its central place to it. In the West there is only one religion and a single style; in India there are various religions, with one and the same style. The change in the West is artistic; there is a transition from the Romanesque to the Gothic. In India there is no change, but rather the maturation of a style and the beginning of a mannerism; the real change is religious: there is a growing tendency toward theism[5] and Buddhism complicates its pantheon and vastly enlarges it. Gothic art is sublime: the cathedral is not the space visited by the divine Presence; rather, it ascends toward it. The sign *non-body* volatilizes the figures and the stone itself is overcome by a spiritual anguish. Gupta art is sensual even in its most spiritual expressions, such as the smiling, contemplative face of Vishnu or Buddha. The Gothic is an arrow or a tormented spiral; the Gupta style loves the curve that winds back upon itself or opens out and palpitates: fruits, hips, breasts.

The post-Gupta sensual spirituality—such as we see it at Ajanta, Elephanta, and Mahabalipuram—is already so sophisticated a style that it soon leads to the Baroque: the immense, phantasmagorical erotic cathedrals of Khajuraho and Konarak. The same thing happens in reverse with the flamboyant Gothic. In both styles the sinuous triumphs, and the line twists and untwists and twists again, creating a dense vegetation. This is the temple as a forest made up more of branches and leaves than of trunks: a superfluous proliferation either of the spiritual or of the corporeal. In both there is a mystico-erotic treatment of

---

[5] The term theism is ambiguous. In this case it in no wise implies the notion of a single god who is the Creator, as in the West.

motifs. Sculptured flames: the sign of the *non-body* is all-powerful in the flamboyant Gothic; the sign of the *body* covers the walls of the Hindu temples.

All these similarities and contrasts can be summed up in one: that between primitive Buddhism and the Protestant Reformation. Two religions without an artistic style of their own: the one because it had not yet created one, and the other because it had rejected what Roman Catholicism offered it. However austere it may be, a religion without a liturgy, without symbols, temples, or altars is not a religion. Therefore, primitive Buddhism used the style that was close at hand and modified it as best it could; Protestantism did the same. Although the sanctuaries of primitive Buddhism have not survived, the testimony of literary texts and archaeology gives us a fairly good idea of what they were like.[6] They could not have been too different from Protestant churches: the same sobriety and simplicity; the same horror of realistic images of the Crucified and the Illuminated; the same veneration for abstract symbols—the cross and the wheel, the book and the tree. This brief description of the development of Indian Buddhist art and medieval Christian art —one of which passes from disincarnation to incarnation and the other from incarnation to disincarnation—shows that at certain times the two of them almost completely coincide. But this is an accidental resemblance: each religion follows its own path and does not intersect the other either in time or in space. Each one traces a spiral without knowing that it is the reverse image of what the other is tracing, as if this were a more perfect and more complex instance of the play of symmetries that Lévi-Strauss has discovered in the mythological system of the Indians of the Americas. The conclusion we may draw from all this

---

[6] See *Histoire du bouddhisme indien*, by Etienne Lamotte (Louvain, 1958).

seems apparent: if these two religions have no contact with each other in history, they nonetheless intersect in these pages. And they intersect because the spirit of all men, in all times, is the theater of the dialogue between the sign *body* and the sign *nonbody*. This dialogue *is* man.

The following schematic drawing shows the relationships—similarities and oppositions—between medieval Christian art and Indian Buddhist art:

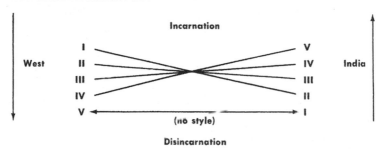

The Roman numerals in the left-hand column (the West) designate: I. the formative (post-Carolingian) period; II. the Romanesque; III. the Gothic; IV. the flamboyant Gothic; and V. the Protestant Reformation (with no style of its own). In the right-hand column (India) the Roman numerals designate: I. primitive Buddhism (without a style of its own); II. the formative (post-Maurya) period; III. the art of Muttra, Sanchi, Andhra, and Western India; IV. Gupta and post-Gupta; and V. the Hindu Middle Ages.

## THE JUDGMENT OF GOD AND THE GAMES OF GODS

The last and the most extreme expression of the Buddhist "corporization" is Tantrism; the final and most radical phase of Christian sublimation is Protestantism. The parallel between these two religious tendencies is impressive for two reasons: because it is an example of an excessive disequilibrium between the signs *body* and *non-body* and because this disequilibrium again takes the form of an inverse symmetry. The oppositions between Tantrism and Protestantism are much like those between light and shade, hot and cold, black and white. Both confront the insoluble conflict between body and spirit (which is emptiness for the Buddhist) and both resolve it by means of an exaggeration. Protestantism exaggerates the separation between body and spirit, to the benefit of the latter; Tantrism postulates the absorption of the body, also to the benefit of "spirit" (emptiness). Both are ascetic, but in Protestantism repression of the body predominates and in Tantrism reintegration of the body predominates. They are thus two attitudes that engender two obsessive types of sublimation: one moral and utilitarian, the other amoral and mystical.

There is a Hindu Tantrism and a Buddhist Tantrism. The manifestations of the two, whether in the sphere of ritual and contemplative practices (*sādhanā*) or in that of doctrine and speculation, are indistinguishable at times. The relationships between these two tendencies have not been entirely explained, and specialists are still debating whether Hinduism has borrowed from Buddhism (*sāktism* and *sivaism*) or vice versa. What is most probable is that they had a common origin and that they grew side by side simultaneously and never entirely commingled. Nonetheless the most recent opinion tends to substantiate that Tantric Buddhism developed first and influenced Hinduism. According to André Bareau, Tantric Buddhist formulas (*dhāraṇī*) seem to have been translated into Chinese as early as the third century. The pilgrim Hsüan Tsang, who visited India four centuries later, reports that "Buddhist monks of the province of Uddiyana recited the same formulas." The two great centers of Buddhist Tantrism were the region of Uddiyana (the valley of Swat) in Western India, and the present states of Bengal, Bihar, and Orissa in the east. Hindu Tantrism is still practiced in these latter. Although the history of Tantrism remains to be written, it is evident that its two branches stem from a common trunk. The dialogue between Buddhism and Hinduism is transformed in Tantrism into something like a love duet: charmed by the same melody, the two protagonists take the words out of each other's mouth.

Agehananda Bharati observes that Hindu and Buddhist Tantrism have no new speculative features, nothing that is not already in the doctrines of Hinduism and in those of Mahayana Buddhism.[7] The originality of both lies in their practices, and above all in the emphasis they place on the efficacy of these practices: liberation (*mukti/sūnyatā*) is an experience that we may have here and now. Both sects agree that this experience consists in the abolition or fusion of contraries: masculine and feminine, subject and object, the phenomenal world and the transcendental world, this latter an absolute in the form of a fullness of being for the Hindu and ineffable emptiness for the Buddhist. Indian tradition had also spoken, in similar terms, of the abolition or fusion of opposites (*samanvaya*) and the ascent to a state of indescribable delight, not without analogy with that of our mystics: union with the absolute (*ānanda*) or dissolution in emptiness (*samatā*) or a regression to the principle of principles, to the inborn (*sahaja*). The characteristic feature of Tantrism is the decision to abandon the conceptual sphere and that of everyday morality (good works and devotions) so as to enter a veritable "dark night" of the senses. Tantrism preaches a total experience, both carnal and spiritual, which must be felt and lived concretely in the ritual.

Both Buddhist and Hindu Tantrism take up—or more

[7] Agehananda Bharati, *The Tantric Tradition* (London, 1965).

exactly, reincorporate—a very old tradition of orgiastic and fertility rites that probably antedates the arrival of the Aryans in the Indian subcontinent. The cult of the Great Goddess and an ascetic and phallic god, which some scholars identify as a proto-Shiva, had already made its appearance in the civilization of the Indus, as I stated before. This is a subterranean tradition that waters the religious subsoil of India and has continually nourished the official religions, even in our own day. Its position and its function within the religious universe might be compared to those of medieval witchcraft in the West, with certain decided differences. The hostility of official Indian religions toward pre-Vedic cults was far less strong than that of Christianity toward witchcraft; the persistence and the influence of this subterranean current was thus much greater in India than in Europe and continues to be so today. In Western culture witchcraft and the other survivals of paganism were suppressed, or else fused with the corpus of Catholicism in a very attenuated and disfigured form; in India the age-old current not only secretly fed the official religions but even managed to carve out a sphere for itself within them—to the point of becoming, with Tantrism, a legitimate, although eccentric, path for achieving liberation from transmigrations and a state of joy and illumination. The attitudes of Indian and Christian established religions vis-à-vis their respective paganisms (*bodies*) are major and extreme examples of conjunction and disjunction.

It seems pointless to discuss the theme of the similarities between Tantric and Hindu Buddhism at any greater length. It is not pointless, however, to cite an observation of Agehananda Bharati: while the Hindu branch owes Buddhism a great part of its conceptual system and its philosophical vocabulary, the Buddhist branch owes to Hinduism many of the divinities in its female pantheon. This factor suggests that it is wisest to focus our attention on Tantric Buddhism as the other pole of Protestant Christianity. Moreover, Tantric Buddhism and Protestantism were radical and violent reactions to their respective religious traditions—the one against the negation of the sign *body* in Buddhism and the other against its affirmation in Roman Catholicism. For these reasons, and for others that will become evident, I shall refer almost exclusively to Tantric Buddhism in the remarks that follow. But I will also be obliged to deal with the revealing oppositions between the Hindu and the Buddhist attitudes, even at the risk of over-complicating the exposition.

I shall begin by discussing the relationship of Tantric Buddhism and Protestantism with the religious traditions which they both inherit and transform: Mahayana Buddhism in the one case and Roman Catholicism in the other. The Buddhist tradition (I am simplifying, of course) is, in turn, the result of two others: the yoga tradition and that of the Upanishads. The first of these is corporeal and magic, the second speculative and metaphysical. The yoga tradition is probably older, corresponding to a pre-Aryan, aboriginal inheritance; the other is Aryan and is directly linked to the Brahmanical current, of which it is the expression and the criticism. Buddhism made its appearance at the beginning as a criticism of Brahmanism, but it is a criticism which embraces the tradition of the Upanishads, if only to deny it, this tradition being in turn critical and speculative. Within Buddhism the tendency to use reason and yoga, the practice of silent meditation and philosophical disputation, enter into a continuous dialogue: the asceticism of Hinayana yoga is countered by the dizzying Mahayana constructions (or rather destructions); the strict Hinayana philosophical criticism is countered by the soaring meditations of the Mahayana Bodhisattvas. It is a dialectic of conjunction: Buddhism tends to assimilate and absorb what is contrary rather than destroying it utterly. Borne on by the logic of its principles or impelled by the

Indian fondness for suppressing contraries without destroying them, the Mahayana tendency preached the ultimate identity between the phenomenal world and emptiness, between samsara and nirvana. This metaphysical affirmation inevitably provoked a resurrection of the corporeal yoga current, in the form of a reverse asceticism: an eroticism. Thus Tantrism does not depart from Buddhism, nor is it, as has been said, a strange, magic, erotic intrusion which destroys the critical and speculative tradition. On the contrary, faithful to Buddhism, it is a new and more exaggerated attempt to reabsorb the corporeal, aboriginal yoga element within the great critical and metaphysical negation of Mahayana Buddhism.

Tantrism attempts an extreme fusion of the two traditions by way of a reabsorption of the older magic and corporeal element. The Protestant attitude toward Catholicism is the exact opposite. Catholicism is also the product of two traditions: Judaic monotheism and the Greco-Roman heritage. The second contains a speculative, corporeal, and orgiastic element, whereas Judaism is not metaphysical but moral and adores an aniconic god whose very name cannot be pronounced. Protestantism denies—or, in less extreme version attenuates—the Greco-Roman heritage and exalts an ideal image of primitive Christianity which is very close to the severity of Judaic monotheism. In other words: there is a separation of the two traditions and a preference for the anticorporeal and antimetaphysical tendency. Within the religious tradition of India, Buddhism is a sort of Reformation and its criticism of Brahmanism culminates in a separation analogous to that of Protestantism from the Roman Church; nonetheless, the history of Indian Buddhism is a series of compromises, not so much with Hindu orthodoxy as with Hindu beliefs; the last and most thoroughgoing of these compromises is Tantrism. Protestantism, on the other hand, was and is an irreparable break. In the one case a loss of balance through conjunction; in the other a loss of balance through disjunction.

The attitudes toward food are revealing. The general rule of Protestantism is sobriety and an emphasis, therefore, on the simplicity and the nutritive value of food. There are no excessive fasts and no gastronomic orgies; it is a cuisine that is insipid and utilitarian. The Tantric banquet is above all an excess, and its utility, if such a word may be used, is other-worldly. There are two things that characterize the Western meal: the food is served in separate dishes and people are well behaved and reserved at table. Before the altar at the moment of communion, this reserve becomes silent meditation and veneration. In India, food is all mixed up on one plate, either out of asceticism or out of hedonism—the two poles of Hindu sensibility. The relation with food is more direct and more physical than in the West; the Indian eats with his hands (sometimes the plate is a leaf from a tree). Tantrism exaggerates this attitude and in the ritual feast people's table manners are deliberately coarse. This emphasizes the religious character of the act: a return to original chaos, and an absorption of the animal world. In the West the food is simple, and in the East there is an excess of condiments; it is nutritional utility versus a sacramental value, sobriety versus excess; distance and reserve with regard to food, closeness and voracity; a separation of dishes, a confusion of permitted and forbidden foods.

The determination of what is permitted and what is forbidden in the way of food is a violent and clear expression of the dichotomy between Protestant separation and Tantric fusion. The Protestant sacrament is almost immaterial, and unlike the Catholic rite, it accentuates the division between the body and the spirit. The Tantric banquet is a ritual violation of the dietetic and moral prohibitions of Hinduism and Buddhism. Not only do the faithful eat meat and drink alcohol; they also ingest foul substances. The *Hevajra Tantra* is explicit: "With the body naked and with bones as accoutrements, one should eat the sacrament in its foul and impure form." The sacrament is made up of minute portions of human flesh, and the flesh of cows, elephants, horses, and dogs, which the devout must mix, knead, purify, burn, and eat, at the same time ingesting the "five ambrosias." Neither the text nor the commentaries are explicit as to what these "ambrosias" really are: they might be either urine, excrement, semen, and other bodily substances, or the five products of the cow, or finally, the allegorical names of the five senses.[8] Whatever the interpretation of this and other passages, there is no doubt that the texts of the *Tantras*, whether Buddhist or Hindu, make the eating of impure food at the moment of consecration mandatory. Almost all the commentators insist on the symbolic nature of the ingredients, above all if they include excremental substances and human flesh, as is the case in the *Hevajra Tantra*. The commentators emphasize that the texts employ an allegorical language: the names of filthy substances and things really designate ritual objects and spiritual concepts. But the explanation hardly appears valid: in many cases the allegorical relation is precisely the contrary, that is, the names of concepts and ritual objects designate material substances and sexual organs and functions in the ciphered language of the text. For example *bala* (mental power) → *māmsa* (flesh) *kakhola* (an aromatic plant) → *padma* (lotus, vulva) *sūrya* (sun) → *rajas* (menstruation) *bodhicitta* (thought of illumination) → *śukra* (semen). The list could be extended.[9] I do not mean to say that the allegorical language of the *Tantras*

[8] See *The Hevajra Tantra*. Translation and critical study by D. L. Snellgrove (London, 1951).
[9] Cf. *The Hevajra Tantra* and A. Bharati's book, *The Tantric Tradition*, already mentioned, especially the chapter devoted to "the intentional language" (*sandhābhāsā*).

consists only in attributing sexual meanings to words that designate spiritual concepts. The language of the *Tantras* is a poetic language and its meanings are always multiple. It also has a quality that I would call reversibility: each word can be converted into its contrary and later, or simultaneously, turn into itself again. The basic premise of Tantrism is the abolition of contraries—without suppressing them. This postulate brings on another: the mobility of the meanings, the continuous shifting of the signs and their meanings. Flesh is mental concentration; the vulva is a lotus that is emptiness that is wisdom; semen and illumination are one and the same thing; copulation is, as Mircea Eliade emphasizes, *samarasa*, the *identité de jouissance*, a fusion of subject and object, a return to the One.

It is not impossible that the rite may many times have been celebrated exactly as described. There is no use in hiding the nature of Tantric rituals; they are not only repulsive but sometimes downright criminal. In view of the reversibility that I have mentioned, it is pointless to discuss whether we are here confronted with symbols or realities: the symbols are experienced as realities and reality possesses a symbolic dimension—it is a metaphor of the absolute. But if the rite has as its object the attaining of a state of nonduality, either through fusion with being or through dissolution in the universal emptiness, it is also natural that it should attempt by every possible means to radically suppress the differences between the permitted and the forbidden, the agreeable and the filthy, the good and the accursed. The Tantric meal is a transgression. Unlike transgressions in the West, which are aggressions tending to destroy, or to abolish, the contrary, the transgression of Tantrism has as its aim to reintegrate—again, to *reincorporate*—all substances—including filthy ones such as excrement and forbidden ones such as human flesh.

The Hindu *Tantras* refer to the consumption of the five M's, that is to say, the five things forbidden by Brahmin orthodoxy, all of which begin with M: *mada* (wine), *matsya* (fish), *māmṣa* (flesh), *mudrā* (beans?), and *maithuna* (copulation). The last two "ingredients" are strange. Bharati identifies *mudrā* as beans and supposes that the devout attribute an aphrodisiac power to this innocuous food. In the Buddhist rite *mudrā* is the feminine partner, and it probably had the same meaning in the Hindu rite. Another possibility is that *mudrā* designated a drug or a portion of human flesh. The *Hevajra Tantra* justifies this hypothesis since it very clearly mentions human flesh as sacred food, and does so several times. As for drugs: Bharati says that during the rite the devout drank a cup of *vijayā*, which is simply the Tantric name of *bhāṅga*, a potion made with ground *Cannabis indica* dissolved in milk and almond juice. It is very popular in the north of India, especially among holy beggars. It is not clear why copulation is included among the five M's, since it is neither an ingredient nor a food. What is more, and most important, it constituted the central part of the rite. These inconsistencies reveal that the Hindu Tantric tradition underwent a period of confusion and disintegration. . . . The extreme immateriality of the Protestant sacrament emphasizes the separation between spirit and matter, man and the world, soul and body; the Tantric feast is a deliberate transgression, a breaking of the rules, the object of which is to attain the *reunion* of all the elements and all substances, to tear down walls, to go beyond limits, to erase the differences between the horrible and the divine, the animal and the human, dead flesh and living bodies, to experience *samarasa*, the identical flavor of all substances.

Protestant communion is individual, and as I have already said, it has retained only the barest trace of the material, corporeal nature of the sacrament. The Protestant rite tends to commemorate the word of Christ; it is not a re-production of his sacrifice as in the Catholic Mass. In the Tantric ceremony all the castes mingle, the taboos of bodily contagion disappear, the sacrament is communal, clearly material and substantial. Immaterial food and individual communion/extremely material food and collective communion; separation and exaggeration of purity/mingling and exaltation of impurity. The caste system consists of a strict and hierarchical distinction between social groups founded on religious notions of purity and impurity. The higher the caste, the more severe the interdictions concerning sex and food, the greater the separation from the natural world and from other human groups. In the inferior castes the ritual prohibitions are more lax and the risks of contamination through contact with the profane, the bestial, or the filthy, are less. Purity is separation, impurity is union. The Tantric ceremony subverts the social order but it does so not for revolutionary but for ritual purposes: it affirms with even more emphasis than the official religions the primacy of the sacred over the profane. Protestantism was also a subversion of the social and religious order; however, it did not turn the old hierarchies upside down in order to return to the primordial mingling of all with all, but in order to proclaim the freedom and responsibility of the individual. It separated, it distinguished, it traced limits intended to preserve personal awareness and privacy. For the one the result was communality; for the other, individualism. A religious reform, Protestantism became a social and political revolution. A transgression of the religious order, Tantrism never abandons the sphere of symbols and rites: it was not (and is not) a rebellion but a ceremony. The social transgression of Tantrism completes the transgression with regard to food and does so with the same end in view: the conjunction of the signs *body* and *non-body*. The blending of flavors and substances into a single indistinct flavor finds its exact equivalent in the dissolving of castes and hierarchies into a circle of adepts, the image of primordial indistinction.

The first modern references to Tantrism occur in a few scattered reports and memoirs of European travelers and residents. Almost all these reports date from the end of the eighteenth century and the beginning of the nineteenth. They are veiled allusions and, naturally, indignant ones; at other times the tone is more frank and more hostile: excited invective, execration mingled with horror—and with secret fascination. The fact that the authors of these reports were missionaries or civil servants of the British Raj has caused modern opinion to regard them as lies and slanderous fabrications. But there is no reason totally to discard them. They may be partial, but there is a good deal of truth in them. The proof is that they often coincide with the texts. I am thinking in particular of the ritual assassination that some of these reports mention. Although the majority of modern commentators (both European and Hindu) say nothing about it, it is frankly described in the *Hevajra Tantra* and, as I understand it, in several other texts as well. The modern interpreters, following various traditional commentators, attempt to explain the mention of a corpse in the rite— either that of a murdered man or that of a dead man spirited away from the place of cremation—as another example of symbolism, similar to that of the impure substances. The distinction between a symbolic and a literal meaning is familiar to Tantric worshipers. As had to be the case in a system such as this, the distinction takes the form of a ritual division: the adepts "on the right hand" follow the allegorical interpretation, whereas the adepts "on the left hand" apply the text literally. Tantrism "on the left hand" is not only the most radical but actually the most Tantric: I have already said that what counts most in this religious system is not the doctrine but the practice (*sādhanā*). This difference between the rites "on the right hand" and those "on the left hand" is great but not irreconcilable. Everything is real in Tantrism—and everything is symbolic.

Phenomenological reality is more than the symbol of the other reality: we touch symbols when we think we are touching bodies and material objects, and vice versa. By virtue of the same law of reversibility, all the symbols are real and tangible: concepts are bodies and even nothingness has a flavor. It is of no consequence whether the crime is real or figurative: reality and symbol fuse, and as they fuse they disappear.

Unlike the human sacrifices of the Aztecs and other peoples, the Tantric murder, whether real or feigned, is not so much a sacrifice as a ritual transgression. The sacrifice takes the form of an offering or a propitiation; in Tantrism the essential element is the crime, the transgression, the violation of the boundaries between what is permitted and what is forbidden. The *Hevajra Tantra* specifies that the victim of the actual murder must be a good man. Total transgression. The meaning of the act is exactly the opposite of the usual and predominant meaning of such an act in other religions. The same dialectic of transgression and reunion that rules the ingestion of impure foods and the confusion of castes in the circle of worshipers operates here. There is nothing similar in Protestantism. Its dialectic is not that of transgression—a violation that makes contraries overflow their boundaries and brings about their conjunction— but rather that of justice. Not the immolation of a victim, but the punishment of the guilty party. Justice re-establishes the limits that the crime has violated. It is a distribution, a reapportioning of rewards and punishments: a world in which each person occupies his proper place. The notion of sacrifice also refers to different realities and concepts. In Protestantism sacrifice is bloodless and moral; the model of Christian sacrifice is that of God, a voluntary victim: there is no other sacrifice than the sacrifice of ourselves. In the Tantric rite the officiant is the one who sacrifices; in the Christian ceremony the worshiper, imitating Christ, offers himself as a sacrifice. His sacrifice is symbolic; it is a representation of the divine sacrifice. In Protestant Christianity the sacrifice is above all an interiorization of the passion of Christ or its symbolic exteriorization, not in the ritual but in daily life: in the worshiper's labor and his social conduct. The sacrifice ceases to be corporeal. In Tantrism there is a confusion between symbol and reality: the sacrifice may be real or figurative, whereas in Protestant Christianity there is a clear distinction between real blood and symbolic blood. In Tantrism magical, physical values predominate; in Protestantism moral values are supreme.

There is another opposition: the different attitudes toward death, or to be more exact, toward dead people. Although the thought and the presence of death are constantly with Christians, Protestantism soon abolished or attenuated its corporeal representations. Death became an idea, a thought that keeps the Christian awake nights and gnaws at his conscience: it lost its bodily presence and its symbolic representation. All the images, at once sumptuous and terrible, that obsessed medieval artists and those of the age of the Baroque in Catholic countries disappeared. The attitude toward the corpse, if not toward death, was similar to that adopted toward gold and excrement: it was hidden and it was sublimated. The dead man evaporated and death became a moral concept. I do not know whether the idea of metempsychosis aids Indians to bear the reality of death. Dying is a hard thing to face at all times and in all cultures. I fear that the function of this Indian belief is analogous to that of our beliefs: it is a device that protects a man against the horror he feels in the face of the fragility and wretchedness of existence, a projection of his fear of final extinction. Buddha himself condemned those nihilists who preached universal and absolute annihilation. In any case, the attitude of Indians toward the dead is more natural than that of Protestant Christians, but they do not delight in its physical, carnal representation as we Spaniards and Hispano-Americans do—except in Tantrism. The fondness of Mexicans for skeletons and skulls has no rival anywhere in the world except in the Buddhist art of Tibet and Nepal. There is a difference however: our skeletons are a satire on life and the living; theirs are alive and licentious. And there is something else: no image of Spanish and Hispano-American Catholicism, no allegory by Valdés Leal, and no skull by Posada possesses the meaning of the corpse which, according to certain informants, is the center around which the entire rite revolves in certain secret ceremonies, a meaning so real that it becomes hallucinatory. Philip Rawson's definition of the rite is sober and precise enough: "Sexual meditation among the corpses."[10] This is exactly the opposite of the Christian meditation on death and the dead.

The reaction of the first European travelers to Tantric practices is somewhat understandable: the violence of their censure is a reflection of the violence of the transgression. The diatribes of the Christian missionaries are no more passionate than those of the orthodox Brahmins and those of certain members of the Tibetan clergy. Lha lama Yesheö writes in the eleventh century:

> Since the development of rites of sexual union, people couple with no regard for their degree of kinship. . . . The practices of you Tantrist village priests may seem startling to others if they hear of it in other kingdoms . . . but you are more greedy for flesh than falcons and wolves, more libidinous than donkeys and bulls, more avid for decomposition than houses in ruin or the chest of a corpse. You are less clean than dogs and pigs. Having offered excrement, urine, sperm, and blood to pure gods, you will be reborn in [the hell of] a swamp full of putrefied corpses. How dreadful![11]

[10] *Erotic Art of the East*, with an Introduction by Alex Comfort (New York, 1968).
[11] Cited by R. A. Stein, in *La Civilisation tibétaine* (Paris, 1962).

This imprecation expresses the horror of the moral consciousness in the face of Tantrism. Morality—of whatever sort, be it
Buddhist, Christian, or atheist—is dualist: *here* and *there*, good
and evil, right and left. But Tantrism is not immoral: it attempts
to transcend all dualisms and thus not even the adjective amoral
fits it. The Tantric attitude, precisely because it is extremely
religious, is not moral. In the sphere of the numinous there is
no *here* or *there*, no *this* or *that*, no cardinal points or
moral precepts. Tantrism is a superhuman effort to really go
beyond good and evil. This lack of moderation may be mindful
of Nietzsche. But Nietzsche's "nihilism" is philosophical and
poetic, not religious. And it is solitary: the burst of laughter and
the dance of the Superman above the abyss of the Eternal
Return. The center, the heart of Tantrism, is something that
Nietzsche rejects: ritual. Nonetheless, there is no return of past
time without ritual, without incarnation and manifestation of
the sacred date. Ritual is the Eternal Return. There is a contradiction in Nietzsche: the Superman, the "perfect nihilist," is a
god without a religion (a ritual) and without a return; and
there is a contradiction in Tantrism: it is a rite that never leads
into history; it is merely a return, a repetition. Once again: what
in the West is act and history is rite and symbol in India. India
answered the idea of "changing the world" with another idea:
dissipating it, turning it into a metaphor.

Tantrism tends to interpret and act out symbols literally.
This literalness is naïve and terrible, as exact as a mathematical
operation and as hallucinatory as a voyage in a dream. Tantrism
is a system of incarnation of images, and this is why it alternately attracts us and repels us. The Abbé Dubois, who was one
of the first to discuss the customs and practices of India, relates
that in the "infamous feast" of Tantrism, the food was placed
on top of a naked girl lying face up. Many friends and defenders
of Indian civilization have called the abbot a liar. I do not know

which makes me more indignant—Dubois's fury or the hypocrisy of the critics. The celebration of a feast in which a naked girl officiates—and that is the correct word—as the donor of the sacrament should not be criticized but praised. It is the incarnation of an image that appears in the poetry of every age: the body of the woman as an altar, a living table covered with living fruits, sacred and terrible. Novalis said that woman is the most exalted corporeal food: is this not what the Tantric ritual also says, though it does so in literal terms? The hunger and thirst of a holy meal, a feasting in honor of our mortality, a eucharist. During the Surrealist exposition dedicated to eroticism some years ago, there was a similar ceremony: a banquet in which the table was a naked woman. The Surrealists were unaware of the Indian antecedent. Images incarnate.

Like all the rest of Christianity, though much more noticeably, Protestantism lacks really erotic rites. Tantrism is above all a sexual ritual. The ceremony of Christian marriage is public but intercourse between bride and bridegroom is private. The Tantric ceremony consists of public copulation, either by several couples or a single couple in front of the circle of worshipers. It is practiced not with the wife, but with a *yogina* (a female practioner of yogi), in general one from an inferior caste. Among Christians the act is consummated in the bedroom, that is to say in a profane place; the *Tantras* specifically state that it must be celebrated in a temple or some consecrated site, preferably in places where the dead are cremated. Copulation atop ashes: destruction of the opposition between life and death, the dissolution of both in emptiness. The absorption of death by life is the reverse of Christianity; the vanishing of both in a third term, sunyata, is the reverse of Mediterranean paganism. We cannot help but admire this dialectic which, without denying the reality of life and the no less real evidence of death, reconciles them by dissipating them. And it reconciles them at the very height of the carnal act; the moment like a flash of lightning that is the most intense affirmation of time and also its negation. Copulation is the real and genuine union of samsara and nirvana, identity between existence and emptiness, thought and nonthought. Maithuna: two in one, the lotus and the lightning bolt, the vulva and the phallus, the vowels and the consonants, the right side of the body and the left, the world above and the world below.

The union of bodies and of opposing principles is also the realization of the hermaphrodite archetype. Reintegration through emptiness is equivalent to the union of the masculine and the feminine part in each of us. On identifying ourselves with emptiness, we also realize ourselves carnally and psychologically: we regain our feminine side, or our masculine side in the case of the woman. Tantrism takes as its point of departure the idea that in each man there is something feminine and in each woman something masculine. Instead of repressing and separating the feminine in man and the masculine in woman, Tantrism seeks to reconcile the two elements. The images of the Indian gods, even though they are always virile, radiate an almost feminine languor and softness. And though Indian goddesses have full breasts, wide hips, and thin waists, they radiate a gravity, an aplomb, a determination that is masculine. The contrast with the Christian West is marked. The results of our repression of femininity in man and of masculinity in woman have been the oceans of curves and the mountains of muscles in Rubens and the triangles and rectangles of the twentieth century.

Physical love is profane in Christian eyes; Tantrism knows nothing of what we call love, and its eroticism is sacramental. Protestantism accentuates the division between the sacred and the profane, the permitted and the forbidden, the masculine and the feminine; Tantrism aims at the absorption of the profane by the sacred, the destruction of the difference between the permitted and the forbidden, the fusion of the masculine and the feminine. The most extreme opposition has to do with the functions of ingestion and of excretion. The central rule of the Tantric sexual rite has to do with the withholding of sperm, not for moral reasons and even less for hygienic reasons, but because the entire act is aimed at the transmutation of semen and its fusion with emptiness. Thus in Tantrism the retention of semen corresponds to the real or symbolic ingestion of excrement; in Protestantism, rapid ejaculation corresponds to the real or symbolic retention of excrement. Seminal retention implies an eroticization of the entire body, a regression to the infantile games and pleasures that psychoanalysis calls polymorphous, pregenital, and perverse. Rapid ejaculation is the triumph of destructive and self-destructive genital eroticism, leading to frigidity in the woman and frustrated pleasure in the man. Ejaculation is linked to death; seminal retention is a regression to a previous state of sexuality. The triumph of death or regression to the undifferentiated sexuality of childhood: in both cases there is selfishness, fear, scorn of the partner. Disjunction and conjunction vitiate the pleasure principle, harm life in its very center.

Protestantism exaggerated the Christian horror of the body. The cause of our perdition, the decent thing is not to mention it, except in the neutral terms of science. For Tantrism the body is the real double of the universe which, in turn, is a manifestation of the adamantine and incorruptible body of Buddha. It propounds a symbolic anatomy and physiology that would be too lengthy and tedious to explain here. I shall merely say that it conceives of the body as a microcosm with six nodes of sexual, nervous, and psychic energy; these centers (*cakras*), from the genital organs to the brain, are connected by two veins (*rasanā* and *lalanā*). The human body is seen as a mandala which serves as an "aid" to meditation and as an altar on which a sacrifice is consumed. The two veins start at the sacred plexus, in which the penis (*linga*) and the vulva (*yoni*) are located. The first vein runs up the right side and polarizes the masculine aspect; the second runs up along the left side and symbolizes the feminine aspect. *Rasanā* is identified with (com)Passion (*karuna*) and with method (*upāya*); *lalanā* with emptiness and wisdom (*prajñā*). The chain of correspondences ramifies to the point of representing a veritable semantic constellation: *rasanā* (the tongue) → *prāna* (the breath of life) → *vyañjana* (the series of consonants) → the Jamuna River/*lalanā* (a dissolute woman) → *candra* (moon) → *apāna* (exhalation) → *svara* (the series of vowels) → the mother (the river) Ganges. There are many crudely material equivalences and linkages of spiritual concepts and sexual realities: *mahamāmsa* (human flesh) → *alija* (the mystical vowels)/*vajra* (a lightning bolt) → *linga* (penis) → *upāya* (meditation). Two notions of Mahayana Buddhism which are really conceptual, the compassion of the Bodhisattva and the action of thought during meditation (*upāya*), take on a predominant erotic symbolism and become homologues of phallus and sperm; *śūnyatā* (emptiness) and *prajñā* (wisdom) evoke the female sexual organs.

During coitus the couple tries to fuse the masculine and the feminine elements—to transcend the duality. The sexual act is a homologue of meditation and both are homologues of reality, which has been divided up into *this* and *that* but which in and of itself is only empty transparency. A third vein—*avadhūtī*— runs between these two veins. The locus of union and intersection, it is the homologue of the *yogina*, the ascetic-libertine woman who "is neither subject nor object." The union of the two currents of energy in the central vein is realization, consummation. A commentary of the poems of Sahāra and Kānha says: "In the moment of great delight, the thought of illumination is born, that is, semen is produced." The great delight (*mahā-*

*sukha*) is also *sahaja,* the return to the innate. The horizontal union, between the feminine and masculine, corresponds to another union which is vertical: the union of semen (*śukra*) with the thought of illumination (*bodhiccita*). The transmutation is achieved by union with the feminine principle, in a moment which is the apex or conjugation of all energy. Instead of being spent, the drop of semen (*bindu*) thus transubstantiated ascends along the backbone until it shatters in a silent explosion: it is a lotus opening at the top of the skull. "Reflection is Consummation": *bindu* is *bodhiccita,* thought without an object, emptiness. Seminal retention is an alchemical and mystical operation: it is not meant to preserve the relation between body and soul but rather to dissolve the first in emptiness. The repressive disjunction in Protestantism and the explosive conjunction in Tantrism ultimately coincide.

A religious geography lies beside this magic physiology that I have briefly described. "Here in the body are the sacred rivers Jamuna and Ganges, here are Pragaya and Benares, the Sun and the Moon. In my wanderings I have visited many sanctuaries but none more holy than that of my body" (Poem of Sahāra). If the body is earth, the sacred earth, it is also language, and a symbolic language: in each phoneme and each syllable there lies a seed (*bīja*) that emits a vibration and a hidden sense when it is actualized in speech. *Rasanā* represents the consonants and *lalanā* the vowels. The two veins, or canals, of the body are now the masculine and feminine aspects of speech. Language occupies a central place in Tantrism; it is a system of incarnated metaphors. Throughout these pages I have referred to the play of echoes, correspondences and equivalences of the ciphered language of the *Tantras* (*sandhābhāsā*). The ancient commentators referred to this erotico-metaphysical hermeticism as "the twilight language": modern commentators, following Mircea Eliade, call it the "intentional language." But the specialists do not say (or else say it like somebody walking on red-hot coals) that this language is essentially poetic and obeys the same laws as poetic creation.

Tantric metaphors are not only intended to hide the real meaning of the rites from intruders; they are also verbal manifestations of the universal analogy that is the basis of poetry. These texts are governed by the same psychological and artistic necessity that caused our Baroque poets to build a language of their own within the Spanish language, the same necessity that inspired the language of Joyce and the Surrealists: the conception of writing as the double of the cosmos. If the body is a cosmos for Sahāra, his poem is a body—and this verbal body is *śūnyatā*. The closest and most impressive example of this is the *trobar clus* of the Provençal poets. The hermeticism of Provençal poetry is a verbal veil: opaque for the ignorant and transparent for the lover who gazes on the nakedness of the lady. One has to be in on the secret: I say *be in on* it and not *know* it. There must be participation: weaving the veil is an act of love and unraveling it is another. The same thing happens in the case of the hermetic language of the *Tantras:* in order to decipher it, it is not enough to know the key but to make one's way into the forest of symbols, to be a symbol among symbols. Poetry and Tantrism are alike in that they are both concrete, practical experiences.

The language of Protestant Christianity is critical and exemplary, a guide to meditation and action; the language of the *Tantras* is a microcosm, the verbal double of the universe and the body. In Protestantism, language obeys the laws of rational and moral economy and even-handed justice; in Tantrism the cardinal principle is that of wealth lavishly spent: an offering, a gift, and also luxury—goods destined to be consumed or dissipated. The "productivity" of the Tantric language belongs to the realm of imitative magic: its model is nature, not work. In Protestantism there is a separation between language and reality: the Holy Scriptures are conceived of as a collection of moral principles; in Tantrism there is a union of language and reality: scripture is *lived* as a body that is an analogue of the physical body—and the body is *read* as a scripture.

Alongside this "intentional language" are magic formulas composed by the syllables that I have already mentioned apropos of the *rasanā* and the *lalanā* as the symbolic rubrics of the consonants and the vowels. These syllables do not go to make up words and Bharati calls them, in a rather forced way, "morphemes or quasimorphemes." The syllables (*bījas*) combine with each other and form sound units: *mantras*. Neither *bījas* nor *mantras* has any conceptual meaning; nonetheless each is extremely rich in emotional, magic, and religious meanings. In Bharati's view the nucleus of Tantrism, its essence as a rite and as a practice, lies in the *mantras*. They are the heart of the religions of India. The *mantra* is the other face of yoga and, like yoga, it is not intellectual but practical and nondiscursive. It is a means of obtaining certain powers. The recitation of the *mantra*, whether silent or aloud, lays down a bridge between the reciter and the macrocosm, as do the breathing exercises of the yogi. But the *mantra* is above all a ritual instrument, to be used either in collective rites or personal worship. There is another aspect to which specialists, in my opinion, have not paid enough attention: the *mantras* are indicative signs, sonorous signs of identification. Each divinity, each guru, each disciple, each worshiper, each concept, and each moment of the ritual has a *mantra* appropriate to it. The poet Kānha has expressed it better than this complicated explanation I have given: the syllables (*bījas*) clasp the naked ankle of the *yogina* like a bracelet. They are sonorous attributes.

Neither Christian prayers and litanies nor abracadabras and other magic formulas are the equivalent of the *mantras*. Perhaps poetry is, or is rather one of its manifestations—which Alfonso Reyes once called "*jitanjáfora*," the nonconceptual explosion of the syllables, the joy, anguish, ecstasy, the anger, the desire expressed in them. It is a language beyond language, as in the poems of Kurt Schwitters, the interjections of Artaud, the serpentine, feline syllables of Michaux, the ecstatic vowels of Huidobro. No, my comparison is omitting the essential, the element that distinguishes the *mantras* from every sort of Western poetic expression: the Indians do not invent these "sonorous jewels"—the guru passes them on to the disciple. Nor are they poems: they are verbal amulets, linguistic talismans, sonorous scapulars. A symbolic and hermetic language—genital words, phonetic and semantic couplings, jingling *mantras*—versus the verbal simplicity of Protestant Christianity and its neutral and abstract moral vocabulary. A language that distinguishes between the act and the word, and between the signifying sign and what it signifies/language that blurs the distinction between the word and the act, that reduces the sign to a mere signifier, that multiplies and changes the meanings of these signs, that conceives of itself as a game that is identical to that of the universe, in which the right side and the left side, the feminine and the masculine, fullness and emptiness, are one and the same—a language that means everything, and nothing.

The word *Prajñāpāramitā* designates one of the cardinal concepts of Mahayana Buddhism. It is the "supreme wisdom" of the Bodhisattvas and the person who has achieved it is already on the "other shore," on the other side of reality. It is the first and the last emptiness. Both the beginning and the end of knowledge, it is also a divinity in the Buddhist pantheon. There are innumerable images in stone, metal, and wood of Our Lady *Prajñāpāramitā*, and the beauty of some of them is unforgettable. I confess that the incarnation in the majesty of a female body of a concept as abstract as that of wisdom in emptiness never ceases to amaze me. A pure idea and a corporeal image, *Prajñāpāramitā* is also a vision and a sound: it is "a red eight-petaled lotus," made up of vowels and consonants "that arises from the syllable Ah. . . ." It is more: a sound and a color, a word reduced to its luminous vibration, an image of stone in a posture of voluptuous meditation, and a metaphysical concept, *Prajñāpāramitā* is at the same time a woman: the *yogina* of ritual. The female partner in the rite is an initiate, almost always of an inferior caste or an impure profession: the *candali* or the *dombī* (laundress). Kānha says in one of his songs to emptiness: "You are the *candali* of passion. Oh *dombī*, no one is more dissolute than you." *Candali* here means the "mystic heat" of the Tibetans: the union of the sun and the moon, the humor of the woman and the sperm of the man, the lotus of Perfect Wisdom and the lightning bolt of (com)Passion, melted and dissolved in one sudden burst of flame. Phenomenal reality is identical to essential reality: the two are emptiness. Samsara is nirvana.[12]

Within the Tantric system the Buddhist and Hindu branches are opposed in the same way that orthodox or traditional Hinduism and Buddhism are opposed. The first great contrast is that while in Hindu Tantrism the active principle is feminine (*Sakti*), in Buddhist Tantrism it is masculine (the adamantine Buddha, *Vajrasattava*). In Tibetan representations of ritual copulation (*yab yum*), the masculine divinity has a terrible and even ferocious look about him, whereas his partner (*dākinī*) has a fragile, though well-rounded, beauty; in Hindu images, the most

[12] With regard to the poems of Kānha and Sahāra see: *Les Chants mystiques de Kānha et Sahāra*, edited and translated by M. Shabidullah (Paris, 1921). See also the two books of Shashibhusan Das Gupta: *An Introduction to Tantric Buddhism* (Calcutta, 1958) and *Obscure Religious Cults* (Calcutta, 1962). *Buddhist Texts Through the Ages* (London, 1954), a collective work by Edward Conze *et al.*, contains the text of the lovely evocation of *Prajñāpāramitā* and Sahāra's poem.

energetic representation of the active principle, often fierce and terrible as well, is Sakti, the feminine pole of reality. At first glance, the Hindu notion contradicts the ideas about women that most societies have had. Nonetheless, this is not illogical: the absolute (represented by Siva) is the subject absorbed in the dream of its infinite solipsism; the appearance of Sakti is the birth of the object (nature, the concrete world) which rouses the subject from its lethargy. Iconography represents Sakti dancing on the sleeping body of Siva, who half opens his eyes. In Judaism there are not only any number of virile and heroic women; there is also our mother, Eve, who wakes Adam from his dream of paradise and obliges him to confront the real world: work, history, and death. In the Bible story, the woman is created from the rib of the sleeping man, as Sakti is born of Siva's dream and also wakes her companion. Eve and Sakti are nature, the objective world. My interpretation may seem to be farfetched. It is not, but it would not matter if it were: there is another important factor which explains the apparent singularity of saktism.

The reason for attributing to Sakti values such as activity and energy, which may appear to be masculine virtues par excellence —although they really are not—is of a formal nature. It belongs to what we might call the law of symmetry, or correspondence, between symbols: the position of one symbol determines the position of the opposite symbol. In Buddhism, the active principle is masculine (*upāya*) but the consummation of the ritual— the abolition of duality—possesses a marked feminine tonality. The two central metaphysical concepts, *śūnyatā* and *Prajñā-pāramitā*, are conceived of as feminine. The abolition of the duality implies the disappearance of the feminine and masculine poles, but this dissolution in Buddhism has a feminine sign. It could not be otherwise, given the position of the symbols. From the beginning, Buddhism affirmed that the supreme good (nirvana) was identical with the cessation of the ebb and flow of existence, and, in its highest form, with emptiness. In Mahayana Buddhism, emptiness was also represented by the round Zero, the image of the woman. For the Hindu, supreme beatitude is the union with being, with the nondual, the One. The coloration is masculine: the One extolled is phallic; it is the quiet, ecstatic linga, full of itself. The Buddhist conceives of the absolute as an object, and thus converts it into a homologue of the feminine pole of reality; the Hindu thinks of it as a subject and associates it with the masculine pole. Two sacred forms condense these images: the stupa and the linga—the Zero and the One. The activity engaged in to attain the (masculine) One cannot be anything but feminine (*Sakti*). Since activity is masculine, Sakti must express not only femininity in its most ample form—round breasts, a narrow waist, and powerful hips—but this femininity that is full to overflowing with itself must emit effluvia, masculine radiations. The same need for symbolic symmetry explains the femininity of the Buddhas and Bodhisattvas; they are the active masculine principle which has conquered and assimilated passivity. *Upāya* corresponds to *śūnyatā*; Sakti corresponds to Siva. The play of correspondences embraces the whole system. If we attribute the cipher zero to femininity, whether active or passive, and the cipher one to masculinity, which also may be either active or passive, the result will be as follows: in Buddhism 1 (active) → 0 (passive); in Hinduism 0 (active) → 1 (passive). From the point of view of their respective ideals of beatitude, the opposition between Buddhist Tantrism and Hindu is 0 (passive)/1 (passive). The means to achieve these goals have the same antithetical opposition: 1 (active)/0 (active). The inverse symmetry that rules each branch is reproduced in the relations between the two. It is the logic of the system, and doubtless the logic of every symbolic system.

The other opposition is no less radical and affects what is the nucleus of Tantrism, the attitude toward seminal ejaculation, with its polarity between feminine and masculine. Unlike Tantric Buddhism, there is no retention of sperm in Hindu Tantrism. Despite the studies that have been devoted to the subject for more than twenty-five years, the first to mention this fact was Agehananda Bharati in a recent work (*The Tantric Tradition* was published in 1965). Bharati was also the first, and to my knowledge the only one, to treat this antithetical relation in a systematic way. The release of sperm is equivalent to a ritual sacrifice, as can be seen in this passage from a Tantric text (*Vāmamārga*): "[The worshiper], while continuing to mentally recite his *mantra*, abandons his sperm with this invocation: 'On with light and ether, [as if they were] my two hands. I am the triumphant . . . I who have consumed *dharma* and *non-dharma* as the portions of the sacrifice, lovingly offer this oblation into the fire. . . .' " *Dharma* and *non-dharma* seem to me to designate here, respectively, what is permitted and what is prohibited by orthodox Hinduism. The final mention of fire, which is identified with the female body, refers to one of the oldest rituals of India: the fire sacrifice. The Hindu Tantric ceremony reincorporates and revives the Indian tradition. The Vedic religion was based on the notion of ritual sacrifice. This is something, as Bharati aptly observes, that has been the cardinal element of the Hindu religion from the Vedic period to the present. Buddhism, on the other hand, appeared precisely as a criticism of the Brahman ritualism and its obsessive penchant for sacrifice. It is true that in the course of its history it created rituals that rival those of Hinduism, but the notion of sacrifice is not central in them. Buddhism puts the accent on the renunciation of the world; Hinduism conceives of the world as a rite whose center is sacrifice. There is asceticism in the former, and ritualism in the latter; seminal retention and release of sperm.

The inverse symmetry which rules the masculine/feminine, active/passive, being/emptiness polarity is repeated in the attitude toward ejaculation, except that now it is manifested in the form of retention/release, renunciation/sacrifice, interiorization/exteriorization. The process is the same: retention of semen = dissolution of the subject in emptiness (the object); release of semen = union of the object with being (the subject). In this dialectic we encounter the same affirmations and negations that define Buddhism and Hinduism: negation of the soul and the *I* versus affirmation of being (*ātman*); a monism without a subject versus a monism that reduces everything to the subject. Although the opposition between Protestant Christianity and Tantrism is of another order, it takes on the same form of reverse symmetry. The relation can be seen more clearly in the case of the basic physiological functions of ingestion and excretion of the two substances—excrement and semen—and their symbols. The symbolic retention of excrement in Protestant Christianity is the equivalent, in an opposite and contrary sense, of its ingestion in Hindu and Buddhist Tantrism (impure foods). With regard to seminal ejaculation, the attitude of Tantrism is unproductive and primarily religious: retention and release are homologues, the first of dissolution in the supreme emptiness and the second of the union with the fullness of being; in Protestantism the meaning is productive and moral: the procreation of children. In Tantrism copulation is a religious violation of moral rules; in Protestantism it is a legitimate practice (if it is done with one's spouse) which is intended to fulfill the Biblical religious precept. Tantrism destroys morals through religion; Protestantism transforms religion into morals. Sperm in Tantrism is transmuted into a sacred substance that becomes immaterial in the end, either because the sacrificial fire consumes it or because it is transfigured into the "thought of illumination." In Protestantism, semen engenders children, a family: it becomes social and is transformed into action upon the world.

Protestantism called for the free interpretation of sacred books and one of the first problems it had to face was that of the meaning of the sacred text: what do the paradoxes of the Gospels and the frequently immoral myths and stories of the Bible really mean? The Protestant interpretation is a moral and rational criticism of mythic language. Tantrism also accepts freedom of interpretation, but its exegesis is symbolic: it transforms the metaphysics of Mahayana Buddhism into a bodily analogy and thus goes from criticism to myth. Protestant language is clear; the language of the *Tantras* is "the twilight language," an idiom in which each word has four or five meanings at once. Protestantism separates myth and morals; Tantrism fuses morals and metaphysics in a mythical language. Protestantism reduces ritual to a minimum; Tantrism is mainly a ritual. In a penetrating study Raimundo Panikar has shown that Christianity is above all an *orthodoxy* and Hinduism an *orthopraxy*; and although this distinction may not be entirely applicable to Hinayana Buddhism, it is to Mahayana Buddhism. Protestantism and Tantric Buddhism exaggerate the tendencies of their respective religious traditions: there is criticism of the texts and of orthodoxy in the former and ritualization of ideas in the latter. There is concern for public opinion in the former and an obsession with practices in the latter; there is clear language and public discussion in the former and a figurative language and secret ceremonies in the latter. Tantrism is esoteric and the doctrine is transmitted in secret; Protestantism proselytizes openly, through example and through the sermon intended for everyone. The former involves hidden, closed sects, the latter open sects that live in the light of day.

The negation of the body and of the world is transformed

into a utilitarian ethic and social action in Protestantism; the absorption of the body in emptiness culminates in the cult of waste and asocial activity in Tantrism. The one exalts the economical and the useful; the other is indifferent to progress and cancels out social and moral distinctions. The one involves solitary introspection—holdovers and remains of sin and virtue —and a silent confrontation with a terrible, just God: the world as process, judgment, and sentence. Good and evil, the useful and the harmful, like *being* and *non-being*, are empty words, illusions for Tantrism: the yogi is a free man who has gone beyond the dualist trap. Protestantism represents the tribunal of conscience; Tantrism the erotic play of the cosmos within consciousness. There is pessimism, moralism, and utilitarianism in the one, and pessimism, amoralism, and nonproductive contemplation in the other. Protestantism represents an organized social life: the priest marries, heads a family, and his church is in the center of the town; Tantrism represents a mystical individual life: the adept is celibate, has no house, and lives on the periphery of the world. The pastor and the wandering ascetic: the one clean-shaven and dressed in black, occupies himself with philanthropic tasks; the other, with his tangled hair and his naked body covered with ashes, dances and sings mystic, licentious songs in the temples. The Protestant is torn by the opposition between predestination and morality; the Indian religious man is a walking paradox. Retention and transformation of excrement into an economic sign; seminal emission in order to procreate children/absorption of excrement and a refusal of monetary exchange; seminal retention so as to obtain illumination. Death through separation of the sex organs and the face: moral aggressivity and, in the end, rigidity. Death through fusion of the sex organs and the face: autophagy and, ultimately, dissolution. The banker and the beggar: extreme, profane figures representing these two tendencies.

# 4 | Order and Accident

## SEXUAL ALCHEMY AND EROTIC COURTESY

The Sinologist R. H. Van Gulik, to whom we owe various works (among them the triple, intriguing, detective story, *Dee Goong An*), published before his death a fundamental book on sexual life in ancient China.[1] The Dutch diplomat puts forward a new hypothesis concerning the origin of Tantrism: the central idea

---

[1] *Sexual Life in Ancient China* (Leiden, 1961). The book deals with a longer period than that indicated by the title, since it ends in the seventeenth century with the Ming dynasty. One observation in passing: Van Gulik translates the scabrous passages of the Chinese texts into Latin, as if knowledge of this language were a certificate of morality. Snellgrove forbears to translate several fragments of the *Hevajra Tantra* which he considers particularly scatological; fortunately they are few in number. But this latter way of going about things is more serious: almost all of us can get something out of Latin, whereas this is not true when the passage is in Tibetan or hybrid Sanskrit.

—the retention of semen and its transmutation—comes from Taoism. This is not the place to discuss his arguments, nor does my limited knowledge of the subject permit me to take part in the debate. I merely wish to point out that in several Hindu Tantric texts there is mention of *Cīna* (China) and *Mahācīna* (Mongolia? Tibet?) as favored regions for practices of sexual meditation. Bharati cites a curious detail: the offering to Siva of a hair from the pubis of the Sakti, pulled out during the ritual copulation and still wet with semen, is called *mahācīna sādhanā*. But it must not be forgotten that the texts to which I am here referring are recent, whereas Vajrayana Buddhism goes back at least as far as the sixth century A.D. The solution of the problem depends, perhaps, on the solution of another problem: the origin of yoga. Is it pre-Aryan and indigenous to India, as the majority of specialists believe today, or does it come from Central Asia (shamanism) as others believe? The presence of yoga elements in primitive Taoism, first pointed out by Maspero, only increases our perplexity. The origin of yoga is as obscure as that of the idea of the soul among the Greeks. In any case there is one thing that no one questions: the great age and the universality of the belief that the retention of sperm is a saving up of life, a storing up of life. Chastity thus becomes a sort of recipe for immortality. The Chinese alchemical texts and the curious *Bed Treatises* offer more than one analogy with the Indian *Tantras*. These similarities are not coincidences; rather they reveal precise influences, either because they are an Indian borrowing from China (as Van Gulik maintains) or because the interchange was much more complicated: a Chinese influence in India; a re-elaboration within the Indian religious context; and a return to China. Once the relation between the Chinese texts and the Indian ones has been accepted, what I am interested in emphasizing is their differences. These seem to me to be more significant than their similarities.

Chinese eroticism is as old as the four legendary emperors. Erotology, in the specialized sense of the word, is also very old and is related both to alchemy and medicine. Van Gulik mentions six *Bed Treatises* dating from the Han period, all of which have disappeared because of the jealousy of the neo-Confucians and the puritanism of the Manchu dynasty. But texts from the Sui, T'ang, and Ming dynasties have come down to us. The collective names of these little works were *Fang-nei* (literally, "in the bed") and *Fang-shi* ("the subject of the bed"). They were extremely popular books. Abundantly illustrated, they constituted a sort of everyday manual, used principally by newlyweds and bachelors. The literary form is didactic, like that of our catechisms: the question-and-answer method. The persons who figure in the dialogue are usually the mythical Yellow Emperor and a girl who initiates him into sexual secrets. The female speaker is sometimes called *Su-nü*, the Simple Girl, sometimes *Hsüan-nü*, the Dark Girl, and sometimes *Ts'ai-nü*, the Chosen Girl. Although these works are inspired by Taoism, in the beginning the followers of Confucius did not violently oppose their diffusion.

In order to understand the nature of these texts, the basic Chinese conception of society, nature, and sex must be kept in mind. The principle is the same for both Confucians and Taoists: the archetype of human order is the cosmic order. Nature and its changes (*T'ien tao*), the light-and-shadow, heaven-and-earth, dragon-and-tiger duality is the basis of the *I Ching* (*The Book of Changes*), as well as of Confucian ethics and politics, the speculations of Lao-tzu and Chuang-tzu, and the elucubrations of the *yang* and *yin* school. No less important is the age-old idea that man produces semen in limited quantities, whereas the woman produces *ch'i*, the vital humor, in unlimited quantities. Thus man must appropriate *ch'i* and conserve his semen as much as possible. The origin of seminal retention is pragmatic in China, while exactly the opposite is true in India. In the *Bed Treatises* the methods for retaining semen and transforming it into a vital principle are enumerated and described in minute detail. Likewise the propitious days for conception are indicated, generally during the week following the end of menstruation.

Immortality, strictly speaking, is not a Confucian notion. Fan Hsün Tzŭ asks Mu-shu: "Our ancestors said: 'dead but immortal.' What did they mean?" Mu-shu answers:

> In Lu there lived a high dignitary called Tsang-Wen-Chung. After his death, his words remained. This is what the ancient proverb means. I have heard that it is best to build on virtue, then on action, and then on words. This is what we may call immortality. As for the preservation of the family name and the continuing of sacrifices to one's ancestors: no [civilized] society can disregard these practices. They are praiseworthy but they do not give immortality.[2]

Yet the permanence of the family, the society, and the State are a sort of social and biological immortality for Confucius and his disciples. Man is society and society is nature: a biological, historical, and cosmic continuity. For this reason, the *Bed Treatises* have only a secondary value: they are rules of sexual conduct intended to prevent premature old age, preserve male vitality, and guarantee fruitful coitus—erotology as a branch of family morality and, by extension, of good government. It must also be said that the advice in the treatises was really very useful if we remember that the Chinese family was polygamous; what these books basically preached was sensible control of masculine sexuality. The Confucian mistrust of them, later becoming frank

---

[2] *Tso chuan* (Commentaries by Tso on the *Annals of Autumn and Spring*), in *A Source Book in Chinese Philosophy*, compiled and translated by Wing-tsit Chan (Princeton, New Jersey, 1963).

hostility, stemmed from the same preoccupation with the stability and sanctity of the family. The books of erotology were something more than treatises on hygiene: they were manuals of pleasure, an encyclopedia of major or minor perversions, apologies for licentiousness, and, what was worse, for unruly passions. As they were avidly read, not only by men but by women, they disturbed the natural harmony of the relations between the sexes, that is, the subordinate position of the woman.

Taoism, from the beginning, presented itself as an art, or method, of attaining immortality, or longevity at least, along with a state of accord with the cosmos. But as it is primarily a method and only secondarily a philosophy, it is similar to yoga. The similarity is even more evident if we take notice of the fact that both Taoist adepts and practitioners of yoga used certain bodily techniques to "nourish the vital principle," and that breathing exercises were the most important of these. Among the Taoist practices for attaining immortality the most important were doubtless those having to do with the retention of sperm. I have already mentioned the universality of the identification of semen with the vital powers, which is age-old. This idea can become obsessive: in modern India most people believe that every loss of semen, either through copulation or through involuntary emission, shortens one's life span. Many Westerners have the same fear, though it may be an unconscious one. In antiquity, semen was made divine by making it the homologue of the vital principle: it was spirit, a divine, creative power. This belief contributed a great deal to the origin and the development of asceticism: chastity was not only a method of storing up life but also a method of transmuting sperm into spirit and creative power. Is that not the meaning of the myths of the birth of Aphrodite and Minerva? Seminal retention for the Taoist adept was only half the operation: the other half consisted in the appropriation of *ch'i*, which was considered to be the purest manifestation of the *yin* essence. I mean *essence* here more in the material sense than in the philosophical, for it is more a fluid than an idea. From its very beginning Chinese civilization conceived of the cosmos as an order based on the dual rhythm —union, separation, union—of two powers, or forces: heaven and earth, masculine and feminine, active and passive, *yang* and *yin*. Assimilating *yin* (*ch'i*) and uniting it to *yang* (nonejaculated sperm) is the equivalent of converting oneself into a cosmos identical to the outer cosmos, governed by the rhythmical embrace of the two vital principles.

Like Tantrism, and for the same ritual and poetic reasons, Taoism invented a secret system of expressions and symbols. The English critic Philip Rawson describes it as a "sexual cryptography."[3] The difference as compared with Tantrism is this: Tantric symbols and expressions are concepts and obey rigorous distinctions of a philosophical nature; Taoist images are fluid and closer to poetic imagination than to rational discourse. Taoism is not governed by an intellectual dialectic but by the law of the association of images: it is a poetic structure that grows like a plant, a tree. In Tantrism, the human body and that of the cosmos are conceived of as a geometry of concepts, a spatial logic; in Taoism, they are conceived of as a system of metaphors and visual images, a tissue of allusions that perpetually comes unraveled and is continually rewoven. The patron saint of longevity in the Taoist list of saints is Shou Lou: this person appears in paintings and engravings as a smiling centenarian with an enormous head—"full of semen," as Rawson emphasizes—holding a peach (the image of the vulva) in his right hand, with his index finger pressing down on the cleft of the fruit. Tantrism brings us face to face with precise symbols, Taoism with allusive and elusive images. The chain of associa-

---

[3] See *Erotic Art of the East* (New York, 1968).

tions inspired by natural forms is very long and very suggestive: a half-opened pomegranate → a peony → a shell → a lotus → a vulva. Dew, fog, clouds, and other vapors are associated with the female fluid, as are certain classes of mushrooms. The same thing happens with masculine attributes: a bird, a ray of light, a deer, a tree of jade. The image of the human body as the double of the cosmic body appears often in poems, essays, and paintings. A Chinese landscape is not a realistic representation, but a metaphor of cosmic reality: the mountain and the valley, the waterfall and the abyss, are man and woman, *yang* and *yin* in conjunction or disjunction. The *Great Medicine of the Three Mountain Peaks* is to be found in the body of the woman and is composed of three juices, or essences: one from the woman's mouth, another from her breasts, and the third, the most powerful, from the *Grotto of the White Tiger*, which is at the foot of the *Peak of the Purple Mushroom* (the mons veneris). According to Rawson these half-poetic, half-medicinal metaphors explain the popularity of cunnilingus among the Chinese: "The practice was an excellent method of imbibing the precious feminine fluid." Tantric corporeal geography refers to religious sites; it is a guide for the pilgrimages of the devout: sacred rivers such as the Ganges and the Jamuna, holy cities such as Benares and Bodhigaya. In China, the body is an allegory of nature: brooks, ravines, mountain peaks, clouds, grottoes, fruits, birds.

The methods of seminal retention and appropriation of *ch'i* were inseparable from alchemy and the practices of meditation. Van Gulik mentions various alchemical texts in which the operations and the transformations of substances were compared to copulation. One of them, entitled *The Pact of the Triple Equation*, is based on a universal analogy: the transmutation of cinnabar into mercury, that of semen into a vital principle during *coitus reservatus*, and the transformation of the various elements according to the combinations of the hexagrams of the *I Ching*. The principle of "two in one"—in an inverse symmetry to the "one in two" of the androgynous archetype—inspires both alchemy and mystical eroticism everywhere: the concept of the body as the analogical double of the macrocosm has barely been conceived when alchemy stretches a bridge between the two. Even a poet who displayed no particular inclination toward Taoist mysticism, Po Chü-i, wrote a poem on the alchemical embraces of the green dragon (the man) and the white tiger (the woman).

In its extreme forms Taoism also practiced public copulation in the Tantric manner. Not out of libertinage—although this, too, is ascetic—but in order to appropriate the vital principle and win immortality or, as I have stated, longevity. One of the most dramatic episodes in ancient Chinese history is the revolt called the Rebellion of the Yellow Turbans. The name refers to a Taoist sect that succeeded in organizing a vast portion of China into a sort of militant and religious communal social system at the end of the Han period. Although we do not have anything but the accounts of the enemies of the Yellow Turbans, it appears that the movement won the passionate loyalty of the people and of certain groups belonging to the intelligentsia. It is also certain that the rebels were practitioners of sexual Taoist mysticism and practiced collective rites of copulation. The rite has survived in semisecrecy down to the present day. In 1950 the government of the Popular Republic of China discovered and broke up a sect (the *I-kuan-tao*) whose worshipers still practiced the ancient sexual ceremonies of magic Taoism.

Indian eroticism presents no similarities. For the Indians, the three central human activities are pleasure (*kāma*), interest (*artha*), and the spiritual and moral life (*dharma*). Eroticism is part of the first of these. As in the case of the Chinese treatises, the first book, the famous *Kama Sutra*, is not the beginning, but the continuation, and the culmination, of a very old tradition. Although its technical content is similar to that of the Chinese texts—positions, aphrodisiacs, magic recipes, a list of anatomical and temperamental compatibilities—there are marked differences. It is not a treatise on conjugal sexual relations; it embraces the whole gamut of carnal commerce between men and women: the seduction of unmarried girls as well as dealings with courtesans, widows, and married and divorced women. There is another major difference: a whole chapter is expressly devoted to adultery. The theme of the book is frankly pleasure, and stolen sexual delights rather than those enjoyed at home, pleasure conceived of as an art—an art of civilized people. The dominant tone is primarily technical: how to come by sexual enjoyment and how to give it; and aesthetic: how to make life more beautiful and how to make sensations more intense and more lasting. There is not the slightest concern either for health (except as a condition of pleasure), or for the family, or for immortality. Morality and mysticism, politics and religion play no part in this text.

I do not know of any book less utilitarian and less religious than the *Kama Sutra*. The same thing is true of the other texts of Indian eroticism, such as the *Kokasatra* and the *Anangaranga*. None of them mentions seminal retention, although they do recommend that the sexual act be as prolonged as possible, and appropriate advice for doing so is provided. They are books having to do with erotic aesthetics and good bedroom manners: their equivalent, in another context, would be Castiglione's *Il Cortegiano*. The Chinese books were part of medicine, and ancient book catalogues listed them under that heading. The Indian books were a branch of the worldly arts, such as the art of cosmetics and perfumes, archery and cooking, music and singing, dance and mime. There is another important difference; they were not aimed either at the religious man or the head of a family but at the dandy and the rich courtesan. Both types are the heroes of the stories, novels, and poems of the great *kāvya* literature. Louis Renou observes that the treatises on eroticism were very useful for writers, poets, and dramatists, who needed to know the theory of *kāma* as well as that of rhetoric (*alam-kara*) and grammar. All the refined literature of Classic India attests to a very great familiarity with the erotic tradition.[4] These, then, were manuals of sexual technique, books on erotic courtesy, catechisms of indolent, refined elegance: pleasure as a branch of aesthetics.

The comparison between Chinese erotic alchemy and Tantric texts reveals differences of another sort that are no less marked. Alchemy plays an important part in the *Tantras*, and as in Taoism its object is to unite the masculine and feminine fluids. But the union serves different ends in each case. In Tantrism it is a means to attain illumination, and secondarily, certain magic powers (*siddhi*); in Taoism immortality is the essential aim. The goal of the Taoist is to reconquer the natural state because, among other things, being immortal means being reunited with the rhythmic movement of the cosmos, being ceaselessly re-engendered, like the year and its seasons, the century and its years. Taoist quietism is inactive, but not immobile: the wise man is like nature, which imperturbably and tirelessly goes its rounds, ever changing and ever returning to its beginning without a beginning. The ideogram of sexual union in the *I Ching* is *Chi-chi*, with the trigram *K'an* (water, cloud, woman) above and the trigram *Li* (fire, light, man) below. It is a moment and a situation within the natural order: the Chinese does not aspire to immobilize it as the Indian does, but rather to repeat it in the instant indicated by the conjunction of the signs. If the universe is cyclical and fluid, immortality must be a life that ebbs and

---

[4] *L'Inde classique* (Paris, 1953).

flows. Discourse is the way of the West, recurrence the way of China.

The Indian denies the flow of things and the passage of time; all his practices and meditations tend to abolish discourse and recurrence: his aim is to stop the wheel of transmigrations. The Taoist flows along with the flux of the cosmos: to be immortal is to go around the circle once more, and at the same time remain motionless in its center. It is a paradox that is as valuable as the Christian paradox or the Buddhist. And it is incomparably wiser than the mad dash of our progress, that blind race from one unknown point to another that is equally unknown. The Taoist *hsü* is a state of calm, freedom, and nimbleness, untouched by the commotion of the world outside. It is not the emptiness of Buddhism, although it is also a state of emptiness. Rather it is the fluid, the nondetermined, that which changes without changing, that which never stops and yet is motionless. Union, yet distance too, like the fog in a Sung landscape or this line of Su Tung-p'o's: "Boatmen and water birds dream the same dream."[5] They dream the same dream but they are not the same. Three attitudes: the Indian denies the natural time of the Taoist and the historical time of Confucius, and sacrifices them on the altar of emptiness or nonduality; Confucius absorbs natural time and its essence, the *ch'i*, so as to transform it into historical time: family, society, the State; the Taoist denies historical time and culture so as to follow the rhythm of natural time. The differences between the Confucian and the Taoist attitudes are divergences; the differences between them and the Indian attitude, whether religious or profane, is a real opposition that makes the similarities insignificant. The surprising thing is not that there were borrowings from one civiliza-

---

[5] *Su Tung-P'o: Selections from a Sung Dynasty Poet*, translated by Burton Watson (New York, 1965).

tion to the other but that one and the same practice, the retention of semen, was the object of such diametrically opposed elaborations and doctrines.

Tantrism denies historical time and natural time. The conjunction between the signs *body* and *non-body* are equivalent to a disembodiment, despite the exaggerated materialism of its practices. Taoism denies historical time: it aspires to reincorporate itself in cosmic time and be one with the cyclical rhythm of heaven and earth which alternately embrace each other and separate. It is another case of conjunction, although less extreme than that of Tantrism. Less extreme and more fecund. Apart from the Taoist classics, which must be numbered among the most beautiful and profound books of any civilization, this doctrine has been like a secret river that has flowed for centuries. It inspired almost all the great poets and calligraphers and we owe to it the best Chinese painting, not to mention its influence on Ch'an Buddhism. Above all, it was for centuries the counterweight to Confucian orthodoxy: thanks to Taoism, Chinese life was not only an immense, complicated ceremony, a tissue of genuflections and duties. Chuang-tzu was the salt of this civilization—the salt and the open door to the infinite. It is therefore unfair to compare Taoism with Tantrism, which is really only the last phase of Buddhism; the comparison really ought to be drawn between Taoism and the great Mahayana schools (*Mādhyamika* and *Vijñāna*). The Buddhist conjunction is active and deliberate, the Taoist passive and unconscious. Buddhism created a strict logic which is no less complex than modern symbolic logic; Taoism was asystematic and aesthetic. In the Buddhist conjunction the sign *non-body* takes on the logical form of the principle of identity: nirvana is samsara; in the Taoist conjunction skepticism and humor dissolve the *non-body*: it is more poetics than metaphysics, more a feeling about the world than an idea. The inability of Taoism to elaborate systems with the richness and complexity of Buddhism saved it: it did not become immobilized in a dogmatic system and was like "the water of the valley" that reflects all the changes of heaven in its quiet waters. This also prevented it from criticizing itself, denying itself, and transforming itself. It slowly declined until it merged and became one with the coarsest superstitions of the vulgar. Taoism ceased to flow and stagnated.

## ORDER AND ACCIDENT

The Confucian attitude toward sex is moral but not metaphysical. It neither deifies nor condemns the phallus. The body is neither evil nor sinful: it is dangerous. We must control it and moderate it. Control and moderation do not mean repression or suppression but harmony. The model of harmony is the immutable principles that govern the conjunctions and disjunctions of heaven and earth. Virtuous society is governed by the same laws: the emperor is the mirror of the cosmos. If the emperor is the son of heaven, the father of a family is the sun of his house. To regulate the emission of semen and absorb the feminine vital principle is to conform to the universal harmony and contribute to the general health of society. Conjugal copulation is a part of good government, like etiquette, the worship of family ancestors, the imitation of the classics, and the observance of the rites. The primordial essence of man is good because it is no different from the intrinsic goodness of nature. This innate goodness is also called order, whether it be cosmic or social. The sexual act fulfills the goal of the institution of the family—to have sons and educate them—which in turn merely reflects and fulfills the order of nature among men. Procreation and education are phases of the same process. During copulation, on favorable days with the proper woman, crude nature, natural time, is absorbed and transmuted into social, historical nature: sons. Education is the process of socialization and integration of biological offspring into the family and the family into the empire. In both cases it is not a question of changing nature but of returning to the natural order. This is what constitutes what I have called, somewhat inaccurately, transmutation. The passionate and chaotic time of sex is converted into historical, social time. History and society are merely nature that has been beautified and returned to its pristine, primordial state.

I have used the word *history* a number of times in the preceding paragraph. I confess that this is an intrusion of a concept that is foreign to Confucius's system. Let me clarify matters, then, by saying that history must be understood to be culture on one hand, and archetypal antiquity on the other hand. The happy state of antiquity can return if men become as cultivated as their forebears. The word *tê* is generally translated as *virtue*, but according to Arthur Waley, the ancient Chinese also called the act of planting seeds *tê*.[6] Therefore *tê* is power: the inherent possibility of growth. Virtue is innate in man because it is a seed, and as such it requires cultivation. The model of cultivation, that is to say of culture, is the action of nature, the great producer of seeds, the mother of virtues. The transformation of semen into virtuous social life—either because its emission during conjugal copulation engenders sons or because its retention prolongs life—is cultivation rather than transformation. In this sense the sexual act is similar to the other acts of civilized man: in all of them natural time is cultivated and made to coincide with its hidden principle. This principle is *T'ien tao*: the cosmic order.

The central idea behind Confucian thought seems to deny the relationship between the signs *body* and *non-body*. What is

[6] *The Way and Its Power* (London, 1934).

more, one has the impression that these signs are not even present in this vision of the world. In fact, what I have called *non-body* is *tê*, virtue, and for Confucius this virtue is nothing other than nature. As for the body, it also is nature and the producer of *tê*. Everything is reduced to a difference of modes of existence and not of essence: the individual biological body, the family social body, the imperial political body, the body of the cosmos. But the same thing might be said, although in the opposite sense, of Buddhism and Christianity: everything is emptiness and everything is spirit. If we consider the real meaning of *tê*, we notice immediately that it is not nature but culture. The opposite term, corresponding to samsara and to sin, is barbarism, the life of the savage. *Non-body* is culture, the virtuous social life. The relation between the signs is the same as in the other civilizations, although its particular meaning is different. What happens (and this explains the confusion) is that the Confucian *non-body*—and even more markedly that of Taoism—is much closer to the body and to nature than Buddhist emptiness and Christian divinity. For this reason, even if sublimation occurred as in the other civilizations, the process that resulted in imbalance between the signs was different.

In a famous study, Max Weber described the analogies between Protestantism and the Confucian mandarin class. He also pointed out their essential difference: the former transforms the world; the latter enjoys and uses its fruits. But in my opinion the major similarity consists in the transmutation of natural time—excrement in the one case and semen in the other—into historical and social time. This similarity, as will be seen later, conceals a difference. Confucius's conception of society is inspired by the natural production of things through the action of an immutable order. This is the meaning of *tê* and of culture. The virtuous society, culture, is society that produces itself and repeats itself like nature. Nature is reintegrated, semen is reabsorbed, and life is multiplied and regulates itself. Order, control, hierarchy: a harmony that excludes neither inequalities nor punishments. There is no disjunction, as in Protestantism, and the conjunction is never extreme, as in Tantrism. But Confucianism was not invulnerable (no idea and no institution is) to the double onslaught of sex and death. In Confucianism the sublimation is expressed as a neutralization of the signs through a progressive paralysis, an immobility that gives the illusion of movement so as to become more perfect: nature becomes culture and culture in turn puts on the mask of a false nature which then is converted into culture and so on. Each time around, nature is less natural and culture more rigid and formal. China preserves itself through recurrence, but it does not deny itself and therefore it does not go beyond itself. The final petrification was inevitable. Petrification and beginning all over again yet another time: yesterday the First Emperor of the Ch'in and today his reincarnation, Chairman Mao. A total, absolute beginning over again, since it not only embraces the present and the future but also the past—through the burning and destruction of the classics yesterday and through the distortion of Chinese civilization and the imposition of the "Maoist interpretation" of history today. These are maniacal confiscations of the past, ever destined to be confiscated in turn by that power which is both the clearest expression of the future and the abolition of all time: forgetfulness. The process of sublimation in Confucianism was culture: an imitation of nature and of the classics; in Protestantism it was moral repression. The two attitudes are expressed plastically, so to speak, in their opposite reactions to semen and excrement.

In India and China conjunction was the mode of relationship between the signs *body* and *non-body*, and in the West disjunction. In its final phase Christianity exaggerates the separation: the body and nature are condemned in the Protestant ethic. The other pole of the relation (spirit, soul) is something very far removed from the Tao of Lao-tzu, the vacuity of Nagarjuna, or the natural order of confucius: the reign of ideas and incorruptible essences. There is a divorce between heaven and earth: virtue lies in the sacrifice of nature so as to merit heaven. In its final phase, Christianity engenders modern areligious society and shifts from a vertical relationship between the terms to a horizontal one: heaven becomes history, the future, progress; and nature and the body, without ceasing to be enemies, cease to be objects of condemnation and become subjects of conversion. History is not circular and recurrent, as in China; nor is it an interval between the Fall and the End, as in medieval society, nor is it a struggle between equals as in Greek democracy: it is action opening out into the future, a colonization of what is to come.

Ancient Christianity, a twin of Islam in this regard, conceived of historical action as a crusade, a holy war, and the conversion of infidels. Modern Westerners transfer the conversion to nature: they operate on it, against it, with the same zeal and with better results than the crusaders against the Moslems. The transformation of excrement into abstract gold was only a part of the immense task of taming the natural world, of finally dominating contaminated and contaminating matter, of consummating the rout of this potent and rebellious element. The conquest, domination, and conversion of nature has theological roots, although those who today are undertaking it are areligious men of science and even atheists. Contemporary society has ceased to be Christian, but its passions are those of Christianity. Despite the fact that our science and our technology are not religious, they have a Christian stamp: they are inspired by the pious frenzy of the crusaders and the conquistadors, directed today not toward the conquest of souls but of the cosmos. China conceived of culture as the cultivation of nature; the modern

West conceived of it as dominion over it; the one was cyclical and recurrent, the other dialectical: it denies itself each time it affirms itself and each one of its negations is a leap into the unknown.

The West represents extreme disjunction and no less extreme violence. There are bound to be some who will question the first-mentioned trait and observe that our era is *materialist*. Others will say that the violence of the West is no greater than that of the Assyrians, the Aztecs, and the Tartars, the only difference being that it is a creative violence: it has covered the earth with splendid constructions and has populated space with machines. I shall answer briefly. It is true that the thought of the West, and above all its science, has been less and less spiritualist since the sixteenth century. The traditional meaning of the sign *non-body* has slowly changed: it had a religious sense (divinity) at first, then a philosophical one (idealism), later a critical sense (reason), and, finally, a materialist one. This latter deserves an explanation. It would be difficult to call atomic particles or biological cells *ideas* or *spirit*. But they are not objects, things, in the sense of the ancient materialism: they are nodes of relations. We are confronted by materialism, to go on using this imprecise term, which opposes the concrete reality of the sign *body* with the same rigidity as it once did spirit. In order to know nature— in reality in order to dominate it—we have changed it; it has ceased to be a corporeal presence and become a relation. Nature has become intelligible up to a certain point, but it has also become intangible. It is no longer a body: it is an equation, a relation that is expressed in symbols and is therefore identical to thought or reducible to its laws. The scientific solipsism is a variant of the linguistic solipsism. Wittgenstein said of this latter that it was legitimate and coherent: "The world is my world: this is shown by the fact that the limits of language stand for the limits of my world. . . . I am my world." Except that this "I am" is not the body but my language—a language that is less and less mine: the language of science.

The abstract nature of our materialism also shows up in our human sciences. The "social things" of Emile Durkheim and Marcel Mauss are not really objects but institutions and symbols worked out by an entelechy that is called society. It is hardly worth the trouble to cite another example: that of historical or dialectical materialism. The first expression indicates that we are in the presence of a historical matter, made by men. It is not the body: it is history. As for the second: no one has yet been able to explain the relation between matter and dialectic. No: our matter is not corporeal, nor is our materialism carnal. The old spirit has changed its name and address. It has simply lost some attributes and gained others. Psychoanalysis itself is part of the sublimation, and, therefore, of the neurosis, of Western civilization. In fact, the boundaries between neurosis and sublimation are very tenuous: the first traps us in an imaginary blind alley and the second opens up an exit for us that is equally imaginary. The therapy of psychoanalysis is equivalent, in the individual, to collective sublimations. Norman O. Brown cites a sentence of Freud's that saves me from having to continue this demonstration: "Neuroses are asocial structures. They attempt to realize by private means what is realized in society by collective means." These collective means are the sublimations we call art, religion, philosophy, science, and psychoanalysis. But these sublimations, included under the sign *non-body*, also lead societies into blind alleys when the relationship with the sign *body* is broken or debased. This is what happens in the West, not in spite of our materialism but because of it. Ours is an abstract materialism, a sort of Platonism in reverse, as disincarnated as the emptiness of Buddha. It no longer even provokes a response from the body: it has slipped into it and sucks its blood like a vampire. All we need do is leaf through a fashion magazine to see the sorry state to which the new materialism has reduced the human form: the bodies of these girls are the very image of asceticism, privation, and fasting.

The disjunction of the West, unlike conjunction in the East, prevents the dialogue between *non-body* and *body*. For the Christian West, foreign societies were always the incarnation of evil. Whether savage or civilized, they were manifestations of the inferior world, the body. And the West treated them with the same rigor with which ascetics punished their senses. Shakespeare says it straight out in *The Tempest*. The difference in attitudes between the colonization of America by the Hispano-Portuguese Catholics and that of Anglo-Saxon Protestants is only an expression of their basic attitudes toward the body. The possibility of mediation between the *body* and the *non-body* still existed for the Catholicism of the Counter Reformation; the consequence was conversion and interbreeding. For Protestantism the gap was unbridgeable, and the result was the extermination of American Indians or their incarceration on "reservations."

We transfer our aggressive tendencies: it is others who threaten us, pursue us, seek to destroy us. The others are also, and primarily, the Other: gods, natural forces, the whole universe. In every civilization, including the first period of our own (medieval Catholicism), earthquakes, epidemics, floods, droughts, and other calamities were seen as a supernatural aggression. At times they were taken to be the manifestations of the wrath, the caprice, and even the mad joy of the divinities, and at other times as punishments for the sins, the excesses, or the failings of men. One recourse was to placate or buy the benevolence of the deity with sacrifices, good works, rites of expiation, and other practices; another was the transfiguration of the penalty through ethical or philosophical sublimation, as in Sophocles's *Oedipus* or in the vision of Arjuna on the battlefield in which he comes to see Vishnu as the indifferent giver of life and death. Man can reconcile himself with his misfortune in both ways, through rites or through philosophical resignation. This reconciliation, whether illusory or not, had a specific virtue: it inserted misfortune in the cosmic and human order, made the exception intelligible, and gave the accidental a meaning. Modern science has eliminated epidemics and has given us plausible explanations of other natural catastrophes: nature has ceased to be the depository of our guilt feelings; at the same time, technology has extended and widened the notion of accident, and what is more, it has given it an absolutely different character. I doubt that the number of victims of falls from a horse and snake bite was greater, even proportionally, than the number of deaths caused by automobiles that overturn, trains that are derailed, or planes that crash. Accidents are part of our daily life and their shadow peoples our dreams as the evil eye keeps shepherds awake at night in the little hamlets of Afghanistan.

Apart from the individual, everyday accident, there is the universal Accident: the bomb. The threat of planetary extinction has no date attached to it: it may be today or tomorrow or never. It is extreme indetermination, even more difficult to predict than the wrath of Jehovah or the fury of Siva. The Accident is the imminently probable. Imminent because it can happen today; probable not only because gods, spirit, cosmic harmony, and the Buddhist law of plural causality have disappeared from our universe but also because, simultaneously, the confident determinism of the science of the nineteenth century has collapsed. The principle of indetermination in contemporary physics and Gödel's proof in logic are the equivalent of the

Accident in the historical world. I do not mean to say that they are the same: I merely say that in the three cases axiomatic, deterministic systems have lost their consistency and revealed an inherent defect. But it is not really a defect: it is a property of the system, something that belongs to it as a system. The Accident is not an exception or a sickness of our political regimes; nor is it a correctable defect of our civilization: it is the natural consequence of our science, our politics, and our morality. The Accident is part of our idea of progress as Zeus's concupiscence and Indra's drunkenness and gluttony were respectively part of the Greek world and of Vedic culture. The difference lies in the fact that Indra could be distracted with a sacrifice of *soma*, but the Accident is incorruptible and unpredictable.

Converting the Accident into one of the cogs of the historic order is no less prodigious a feat than demonstrating that neither the human brain nor computers can prove that the axioms of geometry and arithmetic—the bases of mathematics and the model of logic—are absolutely consistent. But the consequences are different: Gödel's proof leaves us perplexed; the Accident terrifies us. The sign *non-body* has always been repressive, threatening men with eternal hell, the circle of transmigrations, and other punishments. It now promises us total and accidental extinction without distinguishing between the righteous man and the sinner. The Accident has become a paradox of necessity: it possesses the fatality of necessity and at the same time the indetermination of freedom. The *non-body*, transformed into materialist science, is a synonym for terror: the Accident is one of the attributes of the reason that we adore, the terrible attribute, like the halter of Siva or the lightning bolt of Jupiter. Christian morality has given its powers of repression over to it, but at the same time this superhuman power has lost any pretention of morality. It is the return of the anguish of the Aztecs, without any celestial signs or presages. Catastrophe has become banal and laughable because in the final analysis the Accident is only an accident.

## THE BRIDE STRIPPED BARE BY HER BACHELORS

The internal responses to Western repression have been as violent as the external reactions against its colonial oppression. They assumed bizarre and fantastic forms from the very beginning. Van Gulik emphasizes that an examination of the *Bed Treatises* turns up a very small number of sexual perversions and deviations. Anyone who has read Chinese erotic novels will agree with the Dutch Sinologist. The same is true of the literature and the art of India—be it sculpture, the novel, poetry, or books on erotology. The exception is the Tantric texts, but even in them the bloody scatological rites have as their precise object the reabsorption of the destructive instinct. The relation of conjunction prevented the excessive growth of sadism and masochism in ancient Asia. No other civilization, with the possible exception of the Aztecs, offers an art that rivals that of the West in sexual ferocity. And we differ in one way from the Aztecs: their art was a religious sublimation; ours is profane. When I speak of cruelty, I am not referring to the bloody representations of the religious art of the end of the Middle Ages or of those of the Counter Reformation in Spain: I am referring to modern art, from the eighteenth century to the present. Sade is unique, and he is so because the West has been unique in this respect. The relation between *non-body* and *body* assumes the form of torture and orgasm in European erotic books: death as a spur to pleasure and mistress of life. From Sade to the *Story of O* our eroticism is a funeral hymn or a sinister pantomime. In

Sade, pleasure leads to insensibility: the sexual explosion is followed by the immobility of cooled lava. The body becomes a knife or a stone; matter, the natural world that breathes and palpitates, is transformed into an abstraction: a sharp-edged syllogism that suppresses life and, finally, slits its own throat. It is a strange condemnation: it kills itself and thus comes back to life, only to kill itself again.

In areas less overtly aggressive than the modern erotic novel, violence explodes with the same energy, although with less fantastic cruelty. Consider the fight for free love, sexual education, the abolition of laws that punish erotic deviations, and other campaigns of this sort. What scandalizes me is not the legitimacy of these aspirations but the combative and bellicose stance their proponents adopt. The rights of love, the fight for sexual equality between men and women, the freedom of instincts: this vocabulary is that of politics and war. The analogy between eroticism and combat appears in all civilizations, but in none of them except our own does it take on the form of revolutionary protest. The erotic contest is a game, a spectacle for the Indian or the Chinese; for the Westerner, the war-metaphor immediately takes on a military and political meaning, and is followed by a series of proclamations, regulations, norms, and duties. The fanaticism of our rebels is the counterpart of Puritan severity; there is a morality of dissolution as there is a morality of repression, and both of them make equally exorbitant demands on their proponents.

Our attitude toward sexual deviation is another example. Chinese literature does not deal with the theme of masculine homosexuality at any great length, and when it does, it does so only in passing; as for feminine homosexuality, its attitude is benevolent. It is a matter of vital economy rather than a moral problem: copulation between men is not heinous; it is harmful because if it is practiced to excess the opportunity of appropriating the precious feminine *ch'i* is lost. References to the subject in the literature and the art of India are even scantier, although erotic prints with Lesbian themes are common. It is clear that both civilizations were not unaware of these deviations. If they did not exalt them as the Greeks, the Persians, and the Arabs did, neither did they persecute them with the frenzy of the West. The "heinous sin" is another feature peculiar to Christianity. In Delhi and other cities and towns of Uttar Pradesh and Rajasthan there are musicians and dancers, members of a sect, who wander about the streets and public squares dressed as women. They are itinerant artists who practice male prostitution as a side line. They are present—in fact custom makes their presence almost obligatory—when births or marriages are celebrated, both among Hindus and Moslems. In the Victorian India of our day —which has been deformed by the double heritage of English and Moslem puritanism—nobody talks about them but neither does anybody dispense with their songs and dances when a child is born or somebody in the family gets married. In the West, homosexuals tend to be vindictive and their rites are something like meetings of conspirators and plotters. In the East, another habit that is considered more a hygienic mental and physical practice than an abomination is masturbation. When we deal with sexual practices—whether solitary, hetero-sexual, or homosexual—our tendency is to reform rather than to conform. Discord is the complement of the Accident.

The history of the body in the final phase of Western culture is that of its rebellions. In no other era and in no other civiliza-tion has the erotic impulse manifested itself as a purely or pre-dominantly sexual subversion. Eroticism is something more than a mere sexual urge; it is an expression of the sign *body*. But the sign *body* is not independent; it is a *relationship* and it always has to do with the sign *non-body*, whether it is a move-ment toward it or away from it. This rebellion in the West seems to indicate that the disjunction between the signs has become so extreme that the relation tends to disappear almost entirely. The situation is reminiscent, in a reverse sense, of the Cathar heresy, with its emphasis on chastity and its denial of procreation. Yesterday there was an attempt to dissolve the sign *body*, and today an attempt to dissolve the *non-body*. But does the relation really disappear? I have my doubts in both cases. As for the Cathars: even if we do not consider Provençal poetry to be a ciphered expression of Catharism, as Denis de Rougemont maintains, the influence of this movement on the conception of "courtly love" is obvious. In this poetry, neither of the two signs is negated: the ambiguous exaltation of adultery and the ideal lady, the rite of contemplation of the beloved who allows herself to be seen naked provided she is not touched, and the sort of idealization of *coitus reservatus* (known as *asang*) simultaneously affirm the *body* and the *non-body*.[7] It could not be otherwise: the one cannot live without the other. Their unions and separations are the substance of eroticism—that which distinguishes them from mere sexuality. There is no eroticism without reference to the *non-body*, as there is no religion without reference to the *body*. Pure sexuality does not exist among human beings or, probably, among the higher animals. It is a human myth—and a reality among the lower animal species. The function of eroticism in all societies is twofold: it is a sublimation and an imaginary transmutation of sexuality and thus serves the *non-body*, and it is a ritualization and an actualization of images and thus serves the *body*. The bodily rite comes under the sign of the *non-body*, as can be seen in Tantrism; the erotic image, as we

---

[7] *Asang* was one of the degrees of "courtly love" in which the lovers went to bed together naked, but did not consummate the sexual act. (Cf. *L'Erotique des troubadours*, by René Nelli [Toulouse, 1963].) Nelli sees this as a transposition and a purification of the chivalrous "proof of love."

all know from our own experience, comes under the sign of the *body*. In the image the *body* loses its corporeal reality; in the rite, the *non-body* incarnates. The relation between the two signs continues to exist, whether it is a question of traditional images and collective rites or of individual fantasies and private games. Consequently, if the new sexual morality in fact lacks any reference to the *non-body*, it must be interpreted as a nostalgia for animal life, a renunciation of human culture and therefore of eroticism. This is not the case, however. It is a morality: a new attempt of the *non-body* to slip into the body, detach its image, and convert it into an abstract reality. Catharism was the spirit's aversion toward the body; the new sexual morality is a perversion of the body by the spirit.

It is no less disturbing that the rebellion of the senses has taken the form of a social and political demand. Placing sex on the list of the rights of man is as paradoxical as regulating conjugal copulation through the standards of good government. There is a difference: Confucian good government tended to preserve society and referred to a reality that was at once natural and ideal: heaven and its cycle (*T'ien tao*); sexuality as a right tends to change society and refers to a reality that is merely abstract and ideal. We do not seek sexual freedom in the name of the body, which is not a subject with rights; we change it into a political entity. The erotic movements of other civilizations, such as late Taoism and Tantrism, were religious; in other cases—"courtly love" and Romantic passion are the examples closest to hand—they were born and survived on the frontiers of aesthetics, religion, and philosophy. In the West, eroticism has been intellectual and revolutionary since the eighteenth century. The libertine philosophers were primarily atheists and materialists, and only secondarily sensualists and hedonists. Their erotic philosophy was the consequence of their materialism and their atheism—a part of their polemic against the repressive powers of the monarchy and the Church. The combat between the signs *body* and *non-body* turned into a debate and the struggle shifted from the sphere of images, symbols, and rites to that of ideas and theories. The passage from religion to philosophy and from aesthetics to politics was the beginning of the disincarnation of the body. *The 120 Days of Sodom* is a treatise on revolutionary philosophy, not a manual of sexual good manners such as the *Kama Sutra* or a guide to illumination such as the *Hevajra Tantra*. The ancients knew of the practices that Sade describes, so what was really new was not recording their existence but transforming them into opinions: they ceased to be abominations or sacred rites, depending on the civilization, and became ideas.

The new phenomenon is not eroticism but the supremacy of politics. Religious and philosophical ideas were preached in the past but in a strict sense they were not political ideas. Public action was a matter of morals or of convenience: an art, a technique, or a sacred duty, as in the Roman Republic. All this had little or nothing to do with the conception of politics as theory. Our politics by contrast is fundamentally a theory, a vision of the world. Sade's eroticism is a revolutionary philosophy, a kind of politics: he brandishes aberrant practices the way an orator draws up a long list of the people's grievances against the government. It is true that politics was a central activity among the Greeks, the attribute that distinguished the citizen from the slave and the barbarian. But it was not a method for changing the world. Its aim was individual and collective: in the first place, to distinguish oneself in the eyes of others either by the persuasion of one's virtuous example or the cleverness of one's rhetoric and thus gain fame, achieve renown, and, in short, realize the ideal of the citizen; in the second place, to contribute to the health of the *polis*, whatever meaning is given to *health* and *polis*: the independence of the city or its power, the freedom of its citizens or their happiness. The political doctrines of Plato, Aristotle, and the Stoics are not a theory of the world but the projection of their respective theories into the sphere of society and the State. For the Encyclopedists and later for Marx, theory is not only inseparable from practice, but theory, as theory, is already practice, action on the world. Theory, *simply because it is theory*, is political. In a society such as the Chinese, preoccupied above all else with the preservation of the social order and the continuity of culture—preoccupations which are not exclusively political though they may appear to be so— censorship itself was an imperial function: the throne named ministers and censors as a gardener uses both fertilizer and clippers. Politics was part of cosmology (the law of heaven) and of the art of cultivation. In our society science and culture are expressions of classes or of civilizations: they are history, and, in the last analysis, politics. When I say that politics for us is a vision of the world, I am being a bit inaccurate: our idea of the world is not a vision but a judgment and thus it is also an action, a practice. The image of the world, or rather, *the idea of the world as an image*, has given way to another idea, another image: that of revolutionary theory. Our idea of the world is *to change the world*. Politics is a synonym of revolution.

When they attempted to translate the word *revolution*, the Chinese could find no better expression than *ko-ming*.[8] *Ko-ming* means "change of mandate," and by extension, change of dynasty. Whose mandate? Not that of the people but that of Heaven. The Mandate of Heaven (*T'ien ming*) means that the principle that governs nature (*T'ien tao*) has descended upon a prince. In *The Book of History*, Duke Chou says: "Heaven caused the ruin of the Yin dynasty. They lost the Mandate of

[8] See *Confucian China and Its Modern Fate: The Problem of Monarchical Decay*, Vol. II, by Joseph R. Levenson (London, 1964).

Heaven and we, the Chous, received it. But I do not dare to assert that our descendants will keep it." The method for conserving the mandate is Confucian virtue. Nothing is further from our democratic ideas or from the conception of the right to the throne by blood ancestry. Naturally, this doctrine met with opposition, not from philosophers who were expressing the will of the people (there were none), but from apologists for imperial authority. Ancient China evolved a doctrine which served as the other pole of the asocial and individualist attitude of Taoism. This doctrine, a legalism or realism (*Fa-chia*), can be briefly summarized as follows: since the relation between names and the realities that they designate (*hsing-ming*: forms and names) changes and depends on circumstances, the theory of the immutable laws of heaven (*T'ien tao*) does not apply in any way to the art of governing men; it is incumbent upon the prince to give each name a single meaning and thus govern: once what is good and what is evil, what is useful and what is harmful to the State is defined, rewards and punishments can be doled out justly. Han Fei-tzu exhorts his lord: "Discard the benevolence of Yen [a legendary monarch] and forget the wisdom of Tzu Kung [a disciple of Confucius]. Arm the states of Hsü and Lu so that they may face an army of ten thousand war chariots and then the people of Ch'i and Ching will not be able to treat us as they please, as is the case now."[9] In this way the authority of tradition—the immutable meaning of names—was rejected, and along with it the theory of the Mandate of Heaven: authority has no other origin than the prince, the arbiter of names and of rewards and punishments. The doctrine of the Mandate of Heaven affirms, on the contrary, that names and meanings are immutable: what changes are the princes. If the theory justifies

[9] *Han Fei-tzu: Basic Writings*, translated by Burton Watson (New York, 1964). See also: *Three Ways of Thought in Ancient China*, by Arthur Waley (London, 1939).

the change of regime and also obliges the virtuous man to assassinate the prince who violates his Mandate, it prevents the changing of the system at the same time. Levenson comments: *"T'ien ming* doctrine really was an expression of conflict with the emperor, though a bureaucratic, not a democratic expression . . . a defence of gentry-litcrati in their conflict-collaboration with the emperor in manipulating the state." This is exactly the opposite of Saint-Just's doctrine: when Louis XVI was executed, it was primarily to deal a death blow to the monarchic principle.

In the West, revolution means not only a change of system but also something else, which is unprecedented: the changing of human nature. In medieval Christian society as in others, the transmutation of man was a religious process; not even philosophers, except for those dealing with religious philosophies such as Platonism, dared intervene in this sphere. But Christianity in its decline transferred the traditional mission of all religions to revolutionary parties: today it is they, not grace or the sacraments, who are the agents of the transmutation. This shift coincides with another in the spheres of art and poetry. In the past the primary and ultimate aim of art was the celebration or the condemnation of human life; beginning with the German Romantics and becoming even more energetic after Rimbaud, poetry set itself the task of *changing life.* Social revolution and revolutionary art became religious undertakings, or at least what antiquity always considered the exclusive province of religion. In this dividing up of the spoils of religion, revolution got as its share ethics, education, law, and public institutions: the *nonbody.* Art's share was symbols, ceremonies, images—everything which I have called the incarnation of images: the sublimated, though perceptible, expression of the sign *body.*

The rebellion of the senses, as part of the general change, has sometimes taken the form of social demands and sometimes the form of poetic rebellion—or better stated, the fusion of poetry with philosophical-moral revolt and with eroticism, according to the Romantic and Surrealist conception. This is one of the facets —or, more exactly, one of the roots—of the ambivalence of modern art, perpetually torn as it is between the expression of life, either to celebrate or condemn it, and the reform of life. Artists and poets of the modern era have worked together with revolutionaries at the task of destroying the old images of religion and monarchy, but they could not go along with them in their substitution of pure ideological abstractions for these symbols. The crisis begins with the German Romantics, torn between their initial sympathy for the French Revolution and their corporeal and analogical idealism. We owe to Novalis some of the most luminous maxims on eroticism and the relations between man's body and the body of the cosmos; but he is also the author of one of the most reactionary essays of the period: *Europe and Christianity.* The conflict, far from dying out, has become even more acute in the last fifty years. It is not necessary to call to mind the drama of Surrealism, the suicide of Mayakowski, or the moral martyrdom of César Vallejo. When the Peruvian poet, at the height of his Communist "engagement," castigates the "Bolshevik bishops," he does not reproach them so much for their theology of high bureaucrats as for not having been able to transform the idea of proletarian fraternity into a genuine communion: a rite that has no god but does have sacraments. This was a nostalgia for the symbol incarnated in the Eucharist.

The two revolutions of the West, the French Revolution and the Russian, enthroned the sign *non-body*, and in both of them this sign was transformed into a revolutionary agent and a teacher of society. The rebellion of the senses was sublimated and made into a moral force. In its most radical forms, it was transformed into a fight for erotic rights, either of women or of sexual minorities. In its moderate expressions it was channeled into action in favor of sexual education and hygiene, the securing of more rational legislation concerning monogamous marriage, the adoption of divorce laws, the suppression of barbarous punishments for sexual deviations, and other similar reforms. None of this was or is what our exasperated senses are asking for: they are asking for images, symbols, rites—forms of our desires, of our obsessions that are imaginary yet also real, ceremonies in which these images may be incarnated without ceasing to be images. The new materialism claims, as emphatically as the religions of antiquity, to possess the key to the universe. This may be true, but it is also certain that it has not been able to give us an image of this world or of other worlds. Its universe has no body and its material is as abstract and incorporeal as an idea. Its science tells us more about how the genital organs function than all the *Kama Sutras* and *Bed Treatises* ever have. But it has not given us an eroticism: in its manuals the words *pleasure* and *imagination* have been replaced by *orgasm* and *health*. Its recipes are techniques for preserving sexual power, regulating procreation, cleaning all the cobwebs of fear out of our psyche, and exorcising the phantoms of the father and the mother. They teach us how to be normal, not how to fall in love or be passionate. There is nothing further removed from an art of loving. By explaining how the body is made and how it functions, they have abolished its image. Then there is the popularity of sports, which has created a confusion between vigor and beauty, physical skill and erotic wisdom. The reaction of young people in our day, with their predilection for loud clothes, fantastic adornments, decadent or wild hairdos and make-up, and even personal uncleanliness, is not surprising. It is better to smell bad than to use toilet water advertised over television. . . . The freedom of industrial society is gray; the freedom that makes passion a hygiene is false. The positions of bodies in the

*Kama Sutra* are always shown against an imaginary landscape, the conventional décor of *kāvya* poetry; the backgrounds in contemporary erotology are either awkwardly portrayed or macabre.

Not everything is hygiene and "comfort" in industrial society. Apart from the lack of fantasy and vuluptuousness, there is also the debasement of the body. Science has reduced it to a series of molecular and chemical combinations, capitalism to a utilitarian object—like any other that its industries produce. Bourgeois society has divided eroticism into three areas: a dangerous one, governed by the penal code; another for the department of health and social welfare; and the third for the entertainment industry. Orgasm is the universal goal—one more product of the system, and more hastily consumed and ephemeral than the others. The Protestant ethic sublimated excrement; capitalism has introduced the principle of rational production into the realm of eroticism. In the Communist countries the old Christian morality has been supplanted by a sort of neo-Confucianism that is less cultured and more obtuse than that of the Ch'ings. When I speak of Soviet puritanism, I am referring to the relatively tolerant period inaugurated by Khrushchev. In Stalin's time, the regime experienced a terror no less irrational than that of the Accident: Political Deviation. But the terror of the Accident has been more on the order of a psychological phenomenon, whereas that of Deviation immediately entered the realm of facts. Man's paradises are covered with gibbets. The first rule of a really free education would be to instill a repugnance for all doctrines of "obligatory happiness" in children. In the first half of the twentieth century, the sign *non-body*, not content with adopting the neutral procedures of science and applying the efficient methods of mass production to sexuality, has again donned its old costume of the hangman and intervened in politics, at times as the administrator of the Third Reich and at others as Commissar of the people.

Persecuted by the idolaters of abundance and by revolutionaries, the sign *body* took refuge in art. The remains of the body, that is: a form disfigured by repression and anger, and tortured by the feeling of guilt and irony. In the art of the past the deformations of the human figure were ritual; in our day they are aesthetic or psychological: the aggressive rationalism of Cubism, and the no less aggressive emotionality of Expressionism. It is subjectivity—rational, sentimental, or simply ironic, but always guilt-ridden—taking its revenge. I am not forgetting that there has been a secret tradition of exaltation of the body, from Rousseau and Blake to Matisse, Joyce, and certain poets; nor am I forgetting that every time that it comes to the surface in history, it is repressed or absorbed by the ruling ethic-aesthetic. The truth is that contemporary art has not given us an image of the body: this is a mission that we have turned over to couturiers and public-relations men. This is not a defect of today's art but of our society. Art reveals, celebrates, or consecrates the image of the body that each civilization invents. No, the image of the body is not invented: it springs forth, it ripens like a fruit, it is born like a sun from the body of the world. The image of the body is the double of that of the cosmos, the human response to the universal nonhuman archetype. Each civilization has seen the body in a different way because each one has had a different idea of the world. The body and the world embrace each other or tear each other apart; they reflect each other or deny each other: the virgins of Chartres smile like Cretan maidens, but their smiles are different—they smile at another world, at the other world. The universe unfolds in the body, which is its mirror and its creature. Our era is critical; it has destroyed the old image of the world and as yet has not created another. That is why we do not have a body. We have an art of disincarnation, as in Mallarmé, or an art that howls with laughter and sends a shiver up our spines, as in the painting of Marcel Duchamp. The ultimate image of the Christian Virgin, the ideal lady of Provençal culture and the Great Goddess of Mediterranean culture is *The Bride Stripped Bare by Her Bachelors, Even.* This painting is divided into two parts: at the top is the goddess, turned into a motor; at the bottom are her worshipers, her victims, and her lovers—not Acteon, Adonis, and Mars, but nine puppets wearing the uniforms of policemen, hotel porters, and priests. It is semen, the vital essence of the Taoists, turned into a sort of erotic gasoline which bursts into flame *before* the body of the Bride is touched. From ritual to an electric toy: an infernal piece of buffoonery.

The idea of revolution was the great invention of the West in its second phase. Societies of the past did not have real revolutions but *ko-ming*, changes of mandate and dynasty. Apart from these changes, they experienced profound transformations: births, deaths, and resurrections of religions. In this respect, too, our era is unique: no other society has ever made revolution its central idea. If this second phase of Western civilization comes to an end, as many people believe and as the reality that we all live tells us, the clearest sign that the end is approaching will be what Ortega y Gasset prophetically called "the twilight of revolutions." It is true that we have never had so many; it is also true that none of them fits the Western conception of what a revolution is. Like the first Christians waiting for the Apocalypse, modern society has been waiting for the arrival of the revolution since 1840. And revolution is coming: not the one that we have been waiting for, but another one, each time another one. Faced with this unexpected reality which cheats us, theologians speculate and try to prove, like Confucian mandarins, that the Mandate of Heaven (the idea of revolution) is the same; what is happening is that the prince (concrete revolution) is unworthy of the mandate. But there comes a time when people cease believing in the speculations of theologians. This is what has begun to happen in the second half of our century. We are witnessing the denouement today: revolution against revolution. It is not a reactionary movement, nor is it inspired by Washington: it is the revolt of the underdeveloped peoples and the rebellion of the young in the developed countries. In both cases the idea of revolution has been attacked in its very center, as much as or more than the conservative idea of order.

I have written elsewhere of what must be called "the end of the revolutionary period in the West."[10] I shall merely repeat here that the idea of revolution—in the strict sense of that word, such as it has been defined by modern thought—is undergoing a crisis because its very root, its foundation, the linear conception of time and history, is also undergoing a crisis. Modern thought secularized Christian time and from among the temporal triad—past, present, and future—it crowned the latter the ruling power of our lives and of history. The future has reigned in the West since the eighteenth century. Today this idea of time is coming to an end: we are living the decadence of the future. It is therefore an error to consider contemporary social upheavals as expressions of the (supposed) revolutionary process which history has been said to consist of. Although these disturbances have been unusually violent and will probably be even more violent in the future, they in no way correspond to the ideas concerning what a revolution is or should be that Tyrians and Trojans, from Chateaubriand to Trotsky, had worked out. On the contrary, all these changes, beginning with that in Russia and not excluding the ones that have taken place in China and Cuba, have failed to confirm the theoreticians'

[10] *Alternating Current* (New York, 1973).

predictions: none of them has occurred where it should have and none of the classes and social forces in the forefront of these changes have been what they should have been. Reality is perverse and stubborn: these changes have occurred in different places, among different classes, and with different results. Whatever their ultimate meaning may be, these events give the lie to the linear idea of history, the notion of the human course of time as a process possessed of a logic, in other words, a genuine *discourse*.

The idea of process implies that things happen one after the other, either in the form of sudden leaps and bounds (revolution) or in the form of gradual changes (evolution). Progress is a synonym of process because it is thought that every change results sooner or later in an advance. Both modes of succession, the revolutionary and the evolutionary, correspond to a vision of history as a march toward something—we are not exactly certain where this something is, except that this *where* is better than the situation today, and that it lies in the future. History is envisioned as a continuous, never-ending colonization of the future. There is something infernal about this optimistic vision of history; the philosophy of progress is really a theory of the condemnation of man, who is doomed perpetually to move forward, knowing that he will never arrive at his final destination. This way of thinking is rooted in the Judeo-Christian tradition, and its mythical counterpart is the expulsion from Eden. In the garden of paradise, a present without a single flaw shone brightly; in the deserts of history, the only sun that guides us is the fleeting future. The subject of this continual pilgrimage is not a nation, a class, or a civilization, but an abstract entity: humanity. As the subject of history, "humanity" lacks substance; it is never present in person: it acts by means of its representatives, this people or that, this class or that. Persepolis, Rome, or New York, the monarchy or the proletariat, in turn *represent* humanity at one moment or another of history as a member of the legislature represents his electors, and as an actor represents the character he is playing.

History is a theater in which a single person, humanity, becomes many: servants, masters, bourgeois, mandarins, clergymen, peasants, workers. The incoherent shouting of all these voices turns into a rational dialogue and this dialogue into a philosophical monologue. History is a discourse. But the rebellions of the twentieth century have violated both the rules of dramatic action and those of representation. We have unforeseen irruptions that disturb the linear nature of history: what should have happened has not occurred and what should have happened later happens now. If Chinese peasants or Latin-American revolutionaries are today the representatives of the subject "humanity," who or what do American and European workers, not to mention the Russian proletariat, represent? Both the events and the actors betray the text of the play. They write another text, or rather invent one. History becomes improvisation. This is the end of discourse and rational legibility.

What might be called *the inversion of historic causality* has its counterpart in the breaks in the linear order. I shall cite an example. It used to be supposed that revolution would be the consequence of the contradiction between the forces of production created by capitalism and the system of capitalist ownership. The fundamental opposition was: industrial production/private capitalist ownership. This real, material opposition could be expressed in terms of a logical dichotomy between reason (industrial production) and unreason (private capitalist ownership). Socialism would be the result of economic development; at the same time it would be the triumph of reason over the irrationality of the capitalist system. Necessity (history) possessed the rigor of logic; it was reason incarnate. Both history and reason were identified with morality: socialism was justice.

And, finally: history, reason, and morality became one with progress. But modern revolts, including the Russian one, have not been the consequence of economic development, but of the absence of development. None of these revolts broke out because there was an irreconcilable contradiction between the system of industrial production and the system of capitalist ownership. On the contrary: in these countries the contradiction went through an initial phase and was therefore socially and historically productive. The results of these movements were also paradoxical. In Russia there was a leap from an incipient industrial capitalism to the system of state ownership. By doing away with the stage of free competition, unemployment, monopolies, and other disasters of capitalism were avoided. At the same time, the political and social counterpart of capitalism—free labor unions and democracy—was literally ignored. No longer a consequence of development, socialism has been a method of fostering it. Therefore it has had to accept the iron law of development: the storing up, the accumulation of capital (modestly called "the accumulation of Socialist capital"). Any accumulation brings on the expropriation of plus-value and an exploitation of the workers; the difference between capitalist and "Socialist" accumulation has been that in the first case the workers could group together and defend their interests, and in the second, because of the absence of democratic institutions, they were (and are) exploited by their "representatives." Socialism, which had ceased being synonymous with historical reason, has also ceased being synonymous with justice. It has lost its philosophical dignity and its moral halo. The so-called "historical laws" have disappeared completely. The rationality inherent in the historical process has proven to be merely one more myth. Or, better: a variation of the myth of linear time.

The linear conception of history makes three things necessary. First of all, there must be only one time: a present continually impelled toward the future. Second, there must be only one leading thread: universal history must be considered to be the manifestation of the Absolute in time, the expression of the class struggle or some other similar hypothesis. The third requirement is the continuous action of a protagonist who is also unique: humanity and its successive transitory masks. The revolts and rebellions of the twentieth century have demonstrated that the subject of history is multiple and that it is irreducible to the notion of class struggle as well as to the progressive and linear succession of civilizations (the Egyptians, the Greeks, the Romans, etc.). The plurality of protagonists has also demonstrated that the leading thread of history is also multiple: it is not a single strand but many, and not all of them are straight ones. There is a plurality of personages and a plurality of times on the march toward many *wheres*, not all of them situated in a future that vanishes the instant we touch it.

The decline of the future is a phenomenon that manifests itself, naturally, in the very place where it shone like a real sun: modern Western society. I will give two examples of its decline: the crisis of the notion of an avant-garde in the realm of art, and the violent irruption of sexuality. The extreme form of modernity in art is the destruction of the object; this tendency, which began as a criticism of the notion of the "work of art," has now culminated in a negation of the very notion of art. Things have come around full circle: art ceases to be "modern": it is an instantaneous present. As for sexuality and time: the body has never believed in progress; its religion is not the future but the present.

The emergence of the present as the central value is visible in many areas of contemporary sensibility: it is a ubiquitous phenomenon. Nonetheless, it is most clearly seen in the youth movement. If the rebellion of the underdeveloped countries denies the predictions of revolutionary thought about the logic of history and the universal historical subject of our time (the proletariat), the rebellion of youth dethrones the primacy of the future and discredits the suppositions of revolutionary messianism and of liberal evolutionism: what excites young people is not the progress of the entelechy called humanity but the realization of each concrete human vocation, here and now. The universality of the rebellion of youth is the real sign of the times: *the signal of a change of time.* This universality must not cause us to forget that the movement of youth has a different meaning in each country: negation of the society of abundance and opposition to imperialism, racial discrimination, and war in the United States and in Western Europe; the struggle for a democratic society against the oppression of Communist bureaucracies and against Soviet interference in the "Socialist" countries of Eastern Europe; the opposition to Yankee imperialism and local oppressors in Latin America. But these differences do not blur the most decisive fact: the style of the rebellion of youth rejecting the institutions and the moral and social systems that hold sway in the West. All these institutions and systems go to make up what is called *modernity*, in contrast to the medieval world. All of them are the offspring of linear time and all of them are being rejected today. Their rejection does not come from the past but from the present. The double crisis of Marxism and the ideology of liberal and democratic capitalism has the same meaning as the rebellion of the underdeveloped world and the rebellion of youth: they are the expressions of the end of linear time.

The twilight of the idea of revolution corresponds to the rapidity with which revolutionary movements are being transformed into rigid systems. The best definition I know of this process came from a guerrilla in Michoacán: "All revolutions degenerate into governments." The situation of the other heir of Christianity, art, is no better. But its prostration is not a consequence of the intolerant rigidity of a system but of the promiscuity of its various tendencies and manners. There is no art that does not create a style and there is no style that does not eventually kill art. By injecting the idea of revolution into art, our era has created a plurality of styles and pseudostyles. This abundance turns into another abundance: that of styles that die aborning. Schools proliferate and propagate like mushrooms until their very abundance finally erases the differences between one tendency and another; movements live about as long as insects do, a few short hours; the aesthetic of novelty, surprise, and change turns into imitation, tedium, and repetition. What is left for us? First, the weapon of dying mortals: humor. As the Irish poet Patrick Kavanagh said to the doctor paying him a visit: "I'm afraid I'm not going to die. . . ." We can sneer at death and thus exorcise it. We can still begin over again.

What excites me about the rebellion of youth even more than their generous but nebulous politics is the reappearance of passion as a magnetic reality. We are not just witnessing another rebellion of the senses: we are confronting an explosion of emotions and feelings. This is a search for the sign *body*, not as a cipher of pleasure (although we must not be afraid of the word *pleasure*: it is beautiful in every language), but as a magnet that attracts all the contradictory forces that haunt us. It is a point of reconciliation of man with others and with himself; it is also a point of departure leading, beyond the body, to the Other. Young people are discovering values that excited figures as different as Blake and Rousseau, Novalis and Breton—spontaneity, the negation of artificial society and its hierarchies, fraternity not only with men but with nature, the ability to be enthusiastic and also to be indignant, and the amazing ability to be amazed. In brief: they are discovering the heart. In this sense the rebellion of youth is different from those that preceded it in this century, with the exception of that of the Surrealists. The tradition of these young people is more poetic and religious than philosophical and political; like Romanticism, with which it has more than one similarity, their rebellion is not so much intellectual dissidence as a passionate, vital, libertarian heresy. The ideology of the young is often a simplification and an acritical reduction of the revolutionary tradition of the West, which itself was scholastic and intolerant. The systematic spirit has infected many groups that arrogantly advocate authoritarian and obscurantist programs, such as Maoism and other theological fanaticisms. Embracing "Chinese Marxism" as a political philosophy and attempting to apply it to industrial societies of the West is at once grotesque and disheartening. It is not the ideology of youth but their attitude, their sensibility more than their thought, that is really new. I believe that in them and through them another possibility for the West is opening up, if only obscurely and confusedly as yet, something that has not been foreseen by ideologists and that only a handful of poets has glimpsed. Something still without form, like a world dawning. Or is this only an illusion of ours and these disturbances the last sparks of a dying hope?

Hearing any participant or eyewitness of the rebellion of young people in Paris in May 1968 is an experience that puts our ability to judge things objectively to the test. In all the accounts I have heard there is one surprising note: the tone of the revolt, at once passionate and disinterested, as if action had been confused with representation: it was like a mutiny that turned into a Festival and a political discussion that turned into a ceremony; epic theater and at the same time public confession. The secret of the fascination that this movement exercised on all those (including the spectators) who were present at its demonstrations lay in its attempt to unite politics, art, and eroticism. There was a fusion of private and collective passion, a continuous ebb and flow between the marvelous and the everyday, the lived act as an aesthetic representation, a conjunction of action and its celebration. There was a reuniting of man with his image: mirror reflections focused in another luminous body. It was a true conversion: not only a change of ideas but of sensibility; more than a change of being, it was a *return to being*, a social and psychic revelation that for a few days broadened the limits of reality and extended the realm of the possible. It was a return to the source, to the principle of principles: being oneself by being with everyone. It was a discovery of the power of language: my words are yours; speaking with you is speaking with myself. It was a reappearance of everything (communion, transfiguration, the transformation of water into wine and of words into a body) that religions claim as their own though it is anterior to them and constitutes the other dimension of man, his other half and his lost kingdom—man perpetually expelled and torn away from time, in search of *another* time, a prohibited, inaccessible time: the present moment. Not the eternity of religions but the incandescence of the instant: a consummation and an abolition of dates. What is the way to enter such a present? André Breton once spoke of the possibility of incorporating an extra-religious sense of the sacred, made up of the triangle of love, poetry, and rebellion, into modern life. This *sacred* cannot emerge from anything but the depths of a collective experience. Society must manifest it, incarnate it, live it, and thus live and consume itself. Revolt as the path to Illumination. Here and now: a leap to the other shore.

And a nostalgia for Festival. But Festival is a manifestation of the cyclical time of myth; it is a present that returns, whereas we live in the linear and profane time of progress and history. Perhaps the revolt of youth is an empty festival, the summons, the invocation of an event that will always be a future event and never a present one, that never will simply *be*. Or perhaps it is a commemoration: the revolution no longer appears to be the elusive imminence of the future but rather something like a past to which we cannot return—yet which we cannot abandon either. In either case, it is not here, but there, always beyond our reach. Possessed by the memory of its future or of its past, by what it was or what it could have been—no, not possessed but rather deserted, empty, the orphan of its origin and its future —society mimics them. And by mimicking them it exorcises them: for a few weeks it denies itself through the blasphemies and the sacrilege of its young people and then affirms itself more completely and more perfectly in the ensuing repression. A mimetic magic. A victim anointed by the ambiguous fascination of profanation, youth is the sacrificial lamb of the ceremony: after having profaned itself through it, society punishes itself. It is a symbolic profanation and castigation and at the same time a representation. The events on October 2, 1968, in the Plaza de Tlatelolco in Mexico City evoked (repeated) the Aztec rites: several hundred boys and girls sacrificed, on the ruins of a pyramid, by the army and the police. The literalness of the rite— the reality of the sacrifice—emphasized in a hideous way the unreal and expiatory nature of the repression: the Mexican powers-that-be punished their own revolutionary past by punishing these young people.

In every case and in every country workers have participated in the movement only as unwilling and temporary allies. This indifference is difficult to explain unless we accept one of the two following hypotheses: either the working class is not a revolutionary class or the revolt of youth does not fit within the classical framework of the class struggle. These two explanations are really one and the same: if the working class is no longer revolutionary, and if social conflicts and struggles become more acute instead of dying out; if the recrudescence of these struggles does not coincide with an economic crisis but rather with a period of abundance; and if a new world class of the exploited has not appeared to take the place of the proletariat in its revolutionary mission, then it is obvious that the theory of class struggle cannot account for contemporary phenomena. It is not that it is entirely false: it is inadequate, and we must seek another principle, another explanation. There are those who will tell me that the underdeveloped countries are the new proletariat. I need hardly point out in reply that the phenomenon of colonial dependence is not new (Marx was familiar with it); moreover, these countries do not constitute a class because of their social, economic, and historical heterogeneity. For this reason they do not have and cannot set up programs and universal plans as an international class, a party, or a church can.

The idea that intellectuals and technicians constitute the new class is more interesting, but unfortunately it has the defect that those groups are neither homogeneous nor can they be considered as a real proletariat—they are not a universal exploited class. As for young people: no dialectical skill and no trick of the imagination can transform them into a social class. From the viewpoint of revolutionary doctrines, what is really almost beyond explanation is the attitude of young people: they have nothing to gain, no philosophy has named them agents of history, and they embody no universal historical principle. This appears to be a strange situation: they are outside the real drama of history in the same way that the Biblical lamb was outside of the dialogue between Jehovah and Abraham. But it no longer seems strange if we observe that, like the rite as a whole, the victim is a representation, or, more precisely, a hypostasis of the revolutionary classes of the past.

The modern world was born with the democratic revolution of the bourgeoisie which, so to speak, nationalized and collectivized politics. By opening to the collectivity a sphere that up until that time had been the closed preserve of a few, it was thought that general politicization (democracy) would immediately result in the distribution of power among everyone.

Although democracy—because of the bureaucratic nature of political parties, economic monopolies, and the manipulation of the means of information—has become a method of a few to control and garner power, we are haunted by the phantoms of the principles, beliefs, ideas, and forms of living and feeling that gave rise to our world. Nostalgia and remorse—this is probably why society indulges in costly and sometimes bloody revolutionary rituals. The ceremony commemorates an absence, or more precisely, it at once convokes, exorcises, and punishes an Absent Guest. The Absent Guest has a public name and another secret name: the first is Revolution and refers to the linear time of history; the other is Festival and evokes the circular time of myth. They are one and the same: the return of Revolution is Festival, the recurring principle of principles. But they do not really return: it is all pantomime, and on another day fasting and penitence. It is the Festival of the goddess Reason—without Robespierre and without the guillotine but with tear gas and television. It is the Return as a verbal orgy, a saturnalia of commonplaces, the nausea that Festival brings.

Or is the rebellion of youth yet another sign that we are living *an end of time*? I have already expressed my belief: modern time—linear time, the homologue of the ideas of progress and history, ever propelled into the future, the time of the sign *nonbody*, of the fierce will to dominate nature and tame instincts, the time of sublimation, aggression, and self-mutilation—is coming to an end. I believe that we are entering another time, a time that has not yet revealed its form and about which we can say nothing except that it will be neither linear time nor cyclical time. Neither history nor myth. The time that is coming, if we really are living a change at times, a general revolt and not linear revolution, will be neither a future nor a past, but a present. At least this is what contemporary rebellions are confusedly demanding. Nor do art and poetry seek anything different, although artists and poets sometimes do not know this. The return of the present: the time that is coming is defined by a *here* and a *now*. It is a negation of the sign *non-body* in all its Western versions: religious or atheist, philosophical or political, materialist or idealist. The present does not project us into any place beyond, any motley, other-worldly eternities or abstract paradises at the end of history. It projects us into the medulla, the invisible center of time: the here and now. A carnal time, a mortal time: the present is not unreachable, the present is not forbidden territory. How can we touch it, how can we penetrate inside its transparent heart? I do not know, and I do not believe anybody knows. . . . Perhaps the alliance of poetry and rebellion will give us a vision of it. I see in their conjunction the possibility of the return of the sign *body*: the incarnation of images, the return of the human figure, radiant and radiating symbols. If contemporary rebellion (and I am not thinking only of that of young people) is not dissipated in a succession of raucous cries and does not degenerate into closed, authoritarian systems, if it articulates its passion through poetic imagination, in the widest and freest sense of the word poetry, our incredulous eyes may behold the awakening and the return to our abject world of that corporeal and spiritual reality that we call *the presence of the beloved*. Then love will cease to be the isolated experience of an individual or a couple, an exception or a scandal. The word *presence* and the word *love* have appeared in these reflections for the first and the last time. They were the seed of the West, the origin of our art and of our poetry. In them is the secret of our resurrection.

# Index